The World's Greatest Team

The World's Greatest Team

A Portrait of the Boston Celtics 1957-1969

Jeff Greenfield

A Sport Magazine Book
Random House   New York

Copyright © 1976 by Jeff Greenfield

All rights reserved under International and Pan-American Copyright Conventions.
Published in the United States by Random House, Inc., New York, and simultane-
ously in Canada by Random House of Canada Limited, Toronto.

Library of Congress Cataloging in Publication data
Greenfield, Jeff.
The world's greatest team.
1. Boston Celtics (Basketball team) I. Title.
GV885.52.B67G72   796.32'364'0974461   76–14176
ISBN 0–394–49560–8

Manufactured in the United States of America
9 8 7 6 5 4 3 2
First Edition

For Carrie Carmichael
and
Casey Carmichael Greenfield

Acknowledgments

Dick Schaap, editor of *Sport* Magazine, first turned my interest in sports into a useful means of (occasional) employment. Not only did the assignments for *Sport* help finance the research for this book; they also justified 1,400 hours of television viewing under the rubric of "scholarship."

Marty Bell, former managing editor of *Sport,* matched me with the Celtics after an article I had done on Dave Cowens. He was a source of information, encouragement and good humor.

This book would have been impossible without the help of the Celtic front office; in contrast to other sports organizations I have seen, the Celtics were unwaveringly helpful, open and cooperative. People such as Jeff Cohen, Jan Volk, Mary Whelan, Frank Challant and the Celtics' "voice," Johnny Most, all made my task easier. And Howie McHugh, who was there when the Celtics were born, and who is still there, helped give life to the stories of those early years.

The Celtics themselves—from Red Auerbach to members of present and past teams such as Bob Cousy, Bill Sharman, Jim Loscutoff, Bob Brannum, John Havlicek, Don Nelson, Paul Silas and Dave Cowens— deserve special thanks for their patience.

I had significant help from the Boston *Globe* in researching this story —from Bob Healy and Mike Barnacle, and especially from the intrepid men of the *Globe*'s library. George Collins, Harris Goldberg and the late

Jack Barry—who had covered the Celtics in their formative years, and who was one of the kindest men I have ever met—helped no end. And I must add eternal gratitude to Bob Ryan, the first-rate *Globe* writer who has had the Celtics as his beat for six years, and whose insights and good humor are equaled only by his guts in calling them as he sees them.

Mike Lupica, who was a sportswriter for the *Phoenix* in Boston, and who now covers the Knicks for the New York *Post,* was another source of assistance. I owe him a drink as soon as he becomes old enough to be allowed into a bar.

To Pat Mitchell of WBZ-TV, to her son Mark, and to Regina Puksar, my thanks for their many kindnesses during my erratic travels to and from Boston.

And finally, to my editor, Larry Lorimer, the St. Francis of Assisi Award for eternal restraint in the face of endless provocations and delays, and for his insights into the difference between good intentions and a real book.

I would like to assign all of these kind people full responsibility for any mistakes I might have made in the pages that follow. But some of them are stronger than I am, so the responsibility is mine.

Foreword

This is a book about success. It is about a group of men who did a job better than anyone else working at the same tasks. It is about a philosophy that has worked for more than a quarter of a century: a simple, unremarkable premise about how to win which is rooted in the dazzlingly primitive notion that people who have the same task to do, do it better when they work with each other, and harder than the people they are competing against.

This is, with few exceptions, not a book about foul deeds, backroom back-stabbing, broken promises, sinister conflicts: They no doubt were a part of the Celtics' past—although the evidence is that conflicts on this team have been held to an irreducible minimum. But I have spent a part of the last eight years in the American political process. And what makes that process debilitating is the way that endless ego struggles get in the way of changing things. I watch sports—as a spectator and a writer—because of what happens on the field; because terms such as success and failure, good and bad, can be determined by looking at the playing arena, at the final score, at league standings. And in sports, I like winners. There may be something unfair about wanting to celebrate those who do the best. But since my political life is spent caring more about people on the bottom, I look on sports as my moral holiday.

It is also a book about continuity. The Celtics have been the most successful sports franchise in our time because they have managed to preserve the sense of greatness about themselves. Even in the brief period between dynasty and rebirth —about 1970—the Celtics, in the words of Red Auerbach, "always conducted themselves as champions." In a remarkable achievement for a team that must constantly renew itself with young athletes, the Celtics have passed on a sense of tradition. From a code of dress to a style of play, this team has preserved something which seems to have gone out of our lives everywhere else: a sense of roots, a sense of responsibility to help a team win. Fifteen years ago, John Havlicek was a rookie listening to men like Frank Ramsey and Bill Russell. Now he is teaching Kevin Stacom and Glenn McDonald. This is one reason why so many of the Celtics have gone on to success as coaches, both at the college and professional level.

And it is finally a book about the difference between excellence and megalomania. Celtics such as Bill Russell, K.C. Jones, Bob Cousy and others all sought the best within themselves. But they did not accept the "winning-is-everything" philosophy. They did not throw aside considerations such as decency in their search for victory. Most of them, in fact, had to come to terms with the difference between winning and warring. The men of the Celtics are proof that the Nixonian approach to sports—and to winning—is not a necessary part of the process.

Bill Russell, who along with Red Auerbach was the key figure in the establishment of the Celtics' dynasty, was once asked what the most important accomplishment of his team was. Russell replied:

"We won most of the games we played."

This is a look at why that happened, and who helped it happen.

Contents

Part One
Prologue

1

The Celtic Tradition

The North End of Boston is the hub of the Hub; the two square miles of land that jut out into the harbor contain most of the town's excitement. Just across the Charles River, facing the North End, are two educational giants: Harvard University and the Massachusetts Institute of Technology. Rising from the river on the Boston side is the quaint and very high-priced Beacon Hill section, with its cobblestoned streets, gas lights and genteel sensibility. A few blocks away is Government Center: a mass of new office buildings and an ultramodern city hall. Within this small area are some of the best restaurants in any city: Anthony's Pier 4 and Jimmy's, built out on piers into the bay; Durgin Park; the Union Oyster House; Joseph's; 1814.

But along Causeway Street, close by this old charm and new elegance, is a run-down, seedy neighborhood dominated by North Station, a massive, yellow-brick building, half-hidden by the elevated tracks and highways that surround it on every side. Almost everything about North Station and its environs suggests abandonment, decay, a better time long ago. Canal Street, which runs across the front of the station, is filled with rooming houses; winos sit in the hallways. There are pornographic movies in the nearby theaters, a Golden Haven café, a century-old cigar store, Joe Patti's Sanitary Barber Shop. A block away, along Friend Street, is the New Garden Gym. Prominent boxers once trained at the old Garden Gym, but the sport is moribund now, and the gym is virtually deserted.

Adjacent to North Station, a part of the same complex, is the old Madison Hotel, now called, in a vain attempt at modernity, the Madison Motor Inn or (depending on which sign you read) the Madison Motor Hotel. Its lobby has a vague Art Deco look and a sense of faded grandeur. Years ago it was a good hotel, like the first-class station hotels of England, a convenient place to stay for businessmen and celebrities who came up from New York on fine trains like the Pilgrim and the Colonial. The Madison Grille, once a favorite meeting spot for such visitors, does not open for dinner any more. Today the people with money come by plane and stay at the Sheraton–Boston in Prudential Center, or at the Ritz-Carlton or the Copley Plaza, the two great old-world hotels of Boston.

Inside the train station is a dimly lit bar called the Iron Horse, a bookstore, a vegetable stand, a Boston Bruins pro shop, a newsstand; the only new look is the vending machine dispensing tickets for the state-run lottery. On the dingy green walls are posted notices of reduced train service; the trains are dying here, as in every other big city, and most of the land in back of North Station, where the tracks once ran right up to the building, is now paved over with asphalt to form a giant parking lot holding 1,000 cars.

Built over North Station is the Boston Garden, nearly a half-century old, originally constructed by New York's Madison Square Garden Company, then bought by the Boston

Arena Corporation more than forty years ago. It was designed primarily to accommodate hockey, the dominant winter sport at the time; to this day, when the Garden floor is converted into a basketball court, several hundred of its seats offer obstructed views. Up on the rafters—in whose direction a newcomer's eyes frequently wander as he waits for the roof to collapse of old age—are rails from which the championship pennants of the city's teams are suspended.

When the Boston Bruins, with their half-century and more of National Hockey League play, are competing, two black-and-gold banners hang from the roof, symbolizing two Stanley Cup victories. But when the other Garden team competes, the arena is filled with thirteen green-and-white banners. They stand for the National Basketball Association championships won by the Boston Celtics. Eleven of those titles were won in thirteen years, eight of them in a row. In this neighborhood, this building, this arena that stands abandoned by the present, the banners of the Boston Celtics symbolize the single element of enduring grandeur: the presence of the greatest team in the history of American professional spectator sports.

From 1957 through 1969, the Boston Celtics built a record that is unique in professional sports. Not simply eight consecutive championships, but a team so good that, were it not for an injury to Bill Russell in 1958, they might have won ten in a row. Not simply a burst of adrenaline in the playoffs, but season-long consistency that earned them nine consecutive Eastern Division titles. During those thirteen years, the Celtics won 706 games while losing 299, a remarkable .702 winning percentage.

Compare this achievement with other sports dynasties. The Montreal Canadiens won five straight National Hockey League Stanley Cups (1956–60), and the Detroit Red Wings won the NHL season title seven years in a row (1949–55). Football's Cleveland Browns won a conference title six years in a row during the 1950's but lost the NFL championship as often as they won it, and the reputation of the Green Bay Packers rests on the strength of five NFL titles in seven years, plus victories in the first two Super Bowls.

Only the New York Yankees' record stands as a potential challenge to the Celtics. The Yankees won fourteen pennants in one sixteen-year period (1949–64). Over those years, they won the World Series nine times. But the combination of regular-season titles and playoff victories gives the edge to the Celtics, particularly since the Yankees were not competing in a league that sought to equalize teams by giving first draft choices to the least successful teams. Further, the Yankees usually had the money to buy the best available players; the Celtics achieved their dominance in the face of persistent financial hardship.

Almost as remarkable as the record of the Celtics is their continuity. With the New York Knickerbockers, Boston is one of the two original franchises left from the 1946 founding of the Basketball Association of America (soon to become the NBA) still playing in the original city. They are the only NBA team playing in their original building. More important, in the last twenty-five years, a period in which professional sports has been constantly destabilized by expansion, franchise shifts, new leagues, collapses of teams and leagues, and endless shifts of players, coaches and owners, the Celtics have had two presidents, two general managers, three coaches, and one style of play. And one man, Arnold "Red" Auerbach, has served at times in all three jobs, and is the creator of that style of play. He developed the theory, and acquired the players that brought the Celtics from failure to contention to dynasty.

The Celtics have won without ever fielding a player who led the league in scoring. They have won without the seven-foot center hovering near the basket, an element which experts have come to consider an essential part of any championship team (against the evidence provided by the Celtics themselves) Indeed, they have won by finding a place for the small player who swaps height for speed and skill. They have won by remembering that basketball is not a five-man game, but an eight-, nine- or ten-man game, in which the bench may make the difference between defeat and victory. Year after year, the Celtics have played with members on the bench who were better than the starting five, and whose entrance into the game sparked a scoring burst or defensive pressure that won the game. And the Celtics have won by making a reality of the oldest cliché in sports: teamwork. As a team, they have had on their rosters more than their share of powerful egos, but virtually without exception those egos were subordinated—on the court—to the Auerbach game.

A Celtic fan who woke up from twenty years in a deep sleep not only would find his team at the same old stand, but would see the same philosophy at work. He would see the Celtics attempting to catch the opposition by surprise, breaking downcourt on a fast break the instant the ball changed hands. He would see the ball handler sweep down the middle, with the forwards cruising along the sidelines and a shooter following behind as a trailer, free for an uncontested fifteen-foot jump shot if the opposition raced downcourt to keep up with the break. He would see a player, usually better than one or two of the starting five, sitting on the bench, ready to come into the game and give the Celtics a lift. He would see a center with an aggressive approach to defense, moving beyond the basket area to harass a ball handler into a mistake. Rarely would he see four Celtics clear out a side while some dazzling ball handler went one-on-one against the defense, for such a style of play is antithetical to the basic Celtic concept.

This is the persistent paradox. Basketball is a game in which the most talented youngsters practice one-on-one ball; the playgrounds of the inner-city black ghettoes produce the most flamboyant players, those who often become the stars, the scorers, the focus of their team. But on the most successful competitive team in professional sports history the single mortal sin is individualism; the most pervasive value is individual sacrifice on behalf of the common good. It is as if a major manufacturing corporation preached socialism to its employees. For the Celtics, it has worked. It worked in 1957, when Boston, a perpetual bridesmaid, added two rookies named Bill Russell and Tommy Heinsohn to the starting line-up and won its first championship; in the early 1960's, even after the two starring guards of the Celtics, Bill Sharman and Bob Cousy, retired from play; in the late 1960's, when Boston was seen as a collection of weary old men, unable to keep up with the younger, flashier teams. It worked until the keystone of the Celtic dynasty, Bill Russell, retired from play. Then, after one disastrous year, a new center named Dave Cowens began to lead them back into contention. In the quarter-century of Auerbach's reign as coach or general manager, the team played under .500 ball only *once*.

The Celtic tradition is still working, not only for Boston, but for the men who played with Auerbach's teams and remembered that tradition after they playing days were over. Every member of the 1962 Celtic squad coached after retiring. In all, more than thirty former players have applied what they learned under Auerbach as coaches elsewhere, and current Celtic players like John Havlicek, Paul Silas and Don Nelson are likely to be coaches in the future. As a group, the men who have been part of the Celtic tradition have influenced their sport more than the members of any other team in any other sport in history.

Despite this remarkable achievement, there has been throughout the years a strong undercurrent of doubt about the Celtics. Some critics have argued that their success had nothing to do with philosophy; that they won because of one man, Bill Russell. Yet no other basketball team ever approached the Celtics' achievement even with such dominant players as Wilt Chamberlain and Kareem Abdul-Jabbar. And after Russell retired, Boston only had one losing season. Within four years of his departure, they were champions again.

How the Celtics built their dynasty—and later rebuilt it—is a story in itself. Time after time, Auerbach found players other teams did not want, could not use, and made them a part of his championship teams. Sam Jones came from an all-black North Carolina college; K.C. Jones was considered too inept on offense to play in the pros; Andy Phillip, Arnie Risen, Gene Conley and Willie Naulls each gave the Celtics a few important years as experienced reserves after they had apparently outlived their usefulness. Don Nelson was picked up from the Los Angeles Lakers for the $1,000 waiver price after they had sent him home. Other key Celtics, including Frank Ramsey and Bill Sharman, were acquired by Auerbach's scrupulous—some said unscrupulous—attention to the complexities of NBA draft rules. Indeed, in all the Celtic championship years, Auerbach engineered only one straight player-for-player trade: Bailey Howell for Mel Counts in 1966. His other trade—for the draft choice that brought Bill Russell—involved giving up two All-Stars for a college player who couldn't shoot.

Year after year, against all the odds and often against the experts' predictions, Boston won the championship on the strength of the total team talents, not the prowess of any one man. And it was done in an atmosphere that would have taken the heart out of a less disciplined, less motivated team. Building the world's best basketball team in the city of Boston had about it the quality of a *Twilight Zone* episode in which a man walks down a busy thoroughfare, desperately asking people to notice him, but going unseen and unheard. The Celtics played their game in a city without a basketball tradition, without a basketball constituency; a city whose public schools did not teach or play the sport, and whose newspapers spent years studiously ignoring what was happening. In the dynasty years, the Celtics rarely filled three-fourths of the Boston Garden, and only *after* the collapse and rebuilding of the team in the 1970's did they average more than 10,000 paying spectators a game.

The championship teams were not a box-office success, but the Celtic achievement must be measured by what happened on the court. The difference between the dynasty that was and the dynasty that might have been for other teams—those on which Wilt Chamberlain played, for example—often came down to one game, one quarter, one shot. There are those who choose to see in the string of Boston's championships nothing more than a constant succession of lucky breaks: a lucky bounce off the rim, a crucial misplay by the other team.

"Well," Bob Cousy said recently, looking back on the Celtics' string, "there was a lot of luck involved. But Arnold [Auerbach] *directed* that luck. I give him much more credit for what he did after he won the first few championships than before. At the start of every year, the guys—particularly those who had been through the losing years—knew what it meant to win. And each year, they wanted it again and again."

Consider, in capsule form, the years of the Celtic dynasty, and a pattern emerges; a pattern of a team making for itself the big break, the turning point of a series or game, supplying a player to bring the team back from defeat. For one year, for two, luck might be the right word; for a thirteen-year record of all but unbroken success, the word is achievement:

•*1957*—With Cousy and Sharman settled in the back-court, Frank Ramsey back from military service, and rookies Tommy Heinsohn and Bill Russell, Boston swept to an Eastern Division title and beat the Syracuse Nationals in three straight to reach the NBA finals. But the St. Louis Hawks, with former Celtics Easy Ed Macauley and Cliff Hagan, were far stronger than their sub-.500 mark over the season suggested. Led by superstar Bob Pettit, the Hawks split the first six games. In the seventh, with two minutes to go, they led the Celtics by 4 points. The Celtics scored 6 straight points, but then a pair of free throws by Pettit sent the game into overtime. At the end of the overtime period, the score was still tied. With two minutes left in the *second* overtime and the score still tied, Russell blocked a crucial shot and Ramsey threw up a ridiculous twenty-foot jump shot. It went in. With two seconds left, the Celtics still led by 2. Then it happened—almost. The Hawks' Alex Hannum threw an inbounds pass the length of the court; the ball slammed off the backboard, and Pettit leapt to tip it in . . . and missed. Boston had its first world title. The star of the game, with 37 points and 23 rebounds, was rookie Tom Heinsohn.

•*1958*—Boston had little trouble repeating as division champion, and they faced St. Louis again in the playoff finals. But this time, in the third game, Russell came down hard after blocking a shot. He ripped tendons on both sides of his right ankle, and chipped a bone. Boston won the fourth game with Bob Cousy playing the pivot. But the Hawks' Bob Pettit scored 32 points in the fifth game and 50 points in the sixth to give St. Louis the championship. Suddenly, the Celtics were only ex-champions.

•*1959*—Sam Jones, in his second year, and rookie K.C. Jones began to spell Cousy and Sharman in the backcourt. But it was one of Auerbach's "castoffs," Gene Conley, who came back to Boston after retiring as a major league pitcher, whose help was crucial. In the Eastern playoffs against Syracuse, Russell fouled out in the seventh game. Conley grabbed two key defensive rebounds to preserve a Celtic victory. In the finals, Boston achieved the first four-game sweep ever—against the once mighty Minneapolis Lakers.

•*1960*—It was the Year of Chamberlain. Playing for Phil-

adelphia, he became the first ever to be named Rookie of the
Year and Most Valuable Player in the same season. Still,
Boston finished first in the East, then eliminated Philly in six
games in the Eastern playoffs. Chamberlain helped. He
aimed a punch at Heinsohn, but hit a teammate instead and
injured his own hand. The St. Louis Hawks carried Boston
to seven games, but Boston blew them out in the deciding
contest.

•*1961*—Auerbach said of this team, generally regarded
as the most spectacular Celtic team ever, "They could
have toyed with any of the top basketball teams of the past.
The original Celtics of New York [the famed team of the
1920's] couldn't have beaten this club one game in a hundred." All of the first Celtic championship team was still
around—Sharman, Cousy, Russell, Heinsohn, Ramsey, Loscutoff—plus Sam and K.C. Jones and NYU rookie Tom
"Stach" Sanders. The season and the playoffs were walk-
aways. After winning their division by eleven games, the
Celtics beat Syracuse and then St. Louis in five games. (After
the finals, Hawk coach Paul Seymour suggested the Celtics
vote Russell three playoff shares.)

•*1962*—The departure of Bill Sharman for a coaching job
in the new American Basketball League meant the loss of the
first key member of the Celtics' first championship team. But
Sam Jones filled the backcourt gap, and the Celtics won sixty
games. Facing the Philadelphia Warriors and a Wilt Chamberlain with a *50.4* season scoring average in the first playoff
round, the Celtics battled down to the seventh game. A Sam
Jones jump shot with two seconds left gave the Celtics the
margin of victory. The final series against the Los Angeles
Lakers also went to seven games. This time, with the score
tied and seconds left, the Lakers had the ball. But Frank
Selvy's jumper for L.A. hit the rim and bounced off. Boston
won by 3 in the overtime.

•*1963*—It was an appropriately symbolic transition—

John Havlicek's rookie year, Bob Cousy's last. The Celtics seemed to be getting old. In the first round of the playoffs, the young, hungry Cincinnati Royals, led by Oscar Robertson and Jerry Lucas, fought to seven games. As usual, however, the Celtics won the deciding game. Then they faced the Lakers and built a lead of three games to one. They lost the fifth game at home. In the sixth game, in Los Angeles, they built a big lead on the strength of II straight points by Havlicek in the first half. But in the fourth quarter, Cousy injured his left ankle and left the game. The Lakers battled to within I point. Cousy limped back in, making his last Celtic appearance. With three minutes to play, Heinsohn broke the game open by intercepting a Jerry West pass and driving downcourt for a lay-up. Boston had its fifth straight championship.

•*1964*—K.C. Jones replaced Cousy as a starting guard, and Willie Naulls, obtained from New York, gave Boston relief in the corners. In the Eastern playoffs, K.C.'s defensive skills shut down Oscar Robertson, and the Celtics beat Cincinnati in five games. In the finals, the Celtics faced the Warriors, now relocated in San Francisco. Wilt Chamberlain won a victory of sorts, knocking out Boston's reserve center, Clyde Lovellette, with a shot to the chin. But the Celtics won the series in five games. Boston's sixth straight championship broke the professional sports record. Nothing like it had ever been done before, and it wasn't over.

•*1965*—Frank Ramsey retired for a business career before the season. John Havlicek took his place as the "sixth man." The Celtics posted their best season record of any dynasty year, 62-18. In the Eastern finals, they faced an old rival, Wilt Chamberlain, with a new team, the Philadelphia 76ers. Once again, the series went to a seventh game, and once again the Celtics appeared to have won, carrying a 110–103 lead into the last two minutes. Then Chamberlain scored 6 straight points, and Boston's lead was cut to I with six seconds left. Bill

Russell's in-bounds pass somehow hit a guy wire, and the 76ers took over with a chance to win. Hal Greer was to throw the ball in to Chet Walker. But Greer, harassed by K.C. Jones, arced the ball, and John Havlicek outleaped Walker and batted the ball to Sam Jones. Celtic announcer Johnny Most screamed, "Havlicek stole the ball!" over and over as the final seconds ticked away. In the NBA finals, against an injury-ridden Los Angeles team, the Celtics won their seventh straight title, in five easy games.

●*1966*—Heinsohn had announced his retirement before the season, but Havlicek and Sanders were depended on to take up the slack. In addition, Boston picked up Laker cast-off Don Nelson on waivers just after the season began. The team won fifty-four games but finished second in regular season play to Wilt's 76ers. After nine straight division titles, Boston was in second place. In the playoffs, however, the Celtics beat Philadelphia in five games. Against the Lakers in the finals, Boston almost blew it. With a three–one lead in games, the Celtics lost the next two, then barely held on in the seventh to squeeze out a 2-point victory. Auerbach had his eighth straight title, and at the end of the season he announced his retirement as coach. Staying on as general manager, he appointed Bill Russell to take his place on the bench.

●*1967*—This year the Celtics faced a superior team. They won sixty games, but again lost the division title to the Philadelphia 76ers, whose 68-13 record was the best in NBA history. The Celtics had a new 20-point man in Bailey Howell, obtained in a trade for center Mel Counts; Havlicek was averaging 21, and Sam Jones, 22. K.C. stayed on a year past his planned retirement to help Russell, his old college roommate, adjust to his new role as player-coach. But with Chamberlain easing up on scoring (for the first time in his career he did not lead the league in points), and concentrating on playmaking, Philly was too strong. The 76ers routed the

Celtics in the playoffs in only five games, winning the last contest by 24 points. The championship string was broken at eight, and everyone said the Celtics were finished.

•*1968*—The Boston Celtic team was aging. Sam Jones was thirty-four before the season began, and Russell was approaching the same birthday. Despite the continued hot scoring of Bailey Howell and the backcourt presence of Em Bryant, Philadelphia again beat out Boston for the division title.

In the first round of the playoffs, the Celtics got by the Detroit Pistons after falling behind two games to one. Then they found themselves behind Philadelphia three games to one. No NBA team had ever come back from that kind of deficit. With Havlicek starting at forward, however, the Celtics managed to push Philly to seven games. In the deciding contest, Sam Jones helped Russell on defense by collapsing on Chamberlain, and Philly's shooting guards simply went cold. Boston won, 100–96. Then, with Havlicek playing defense like a madman, they beat the Lakers in six games for the championship.

•*1969*—It had to end; Sam Jones and Russell were thirty-five. Sanders and Howell were over thirty, both slowed by injuries. And with the resurgent New York Knicks in the East, Boston looked as if it might not even make the playoffs, something that had never happened in all of Auerbach's years in Boston.

The Celtics finished fourth, but less stringent qualifying standards allowed them to enter the playoffs. Chamberlain had left the 76ers, who were left without a rebounder; Boston beat them in five games. Against New York, which had eliminated first-place Baltimore in four straight, Boston won in six, thanks to clutch-shooting by Havlicek and an injury to New York star Walt Frazier. Then it was time for a final series against a new, improved Celtic rival: the Los Angeles Lakers with Wilt Chamberlain, Jerry West and Elgin Baylor.

The Lakers won two of the first three games and held a
1-point lead in the fourth with seven seconds to go. Sam Jones
slipped while getting set for the last shot. He threw it up in
desperation, perhaps hoping that Russell could tap in the
rebound. There was one problem: Coach Russell had taken
Player Russell out of the game. Luckily, the shot hit the rim
and bounced in by itself, tying the series at two games apiece.

Both teams won again. Game seven was played in Los
Angeles, and Laker owner Jack Kent Cooke had everything
ready to celebrate L.A.'s first NBA title: the USC marching
band waited in the corridor, and balloons hung from nets in
the rafters. But in the fourth quarter, Boston had a 17-point
lead and Chamberlain took himself out of the game with a
knee injury. L.A. came back, but Coach Butch Van Breda
Kolff refused to put Wilt back in despite his appeals. Then,
in a final touch of irony, ex-Laker Don Nelson threw up a
shot that got a lucky bounce off the rim and went in, to give
Boston its eleventh championship in thirteen years. Over the
summer, Russell unexpectedly announced his retirement,
and the dynasty years were over.

The record, standing by itself, is a fair definition of success.
Achievement in competitive professional athletics can be easily measured: this team, given the same opportunity and
playing by the same rules, won more championships than
any other. There are no "greater" questions to ask about
what happens on the court.

But it is the special pleasure of sports that the statistical
achievements carry with them a set of memories, images that
sustain our affection for the game. The Celtics gave us a
multitude of such images of grace and excellence as:

•Bob Cousy, the first ball-handing magician of the pros,
whipping passes behind his back, drawing opponents with a
feint, then in an instant finding the open man;

•Bill Sharman, methodical as a machine, firing one-handers with the same motion, again and again and again, wearing the opposition down not with the flamboyance of a great move, but with the ceaseless pressure of water dropping on a rock;

•Bill Russell, rising up to reject a shot in the hands of an opponent, changing the flow and pace of the entire game by his defensive presence;

•K.C. Jones, overplaying his man, harassing the best ball handlers in basketball into turnovers, bad passes, forced shots, making the Celtic defense as devastating in the backcourt as Russell made it under the basket;

•John Havlicek, tirelessly racing up and down the court, leading the break, firing the pass ahead, trailing the play for a jump shot, moving without the ball, game in and game out, for forty, forty-five minutes a game.

And more: Sam Jones, using the backboard like a billiard cushion; Heinsohn and Ramsey, driving from the corners; Sanders, intimidating men half a foot taller. At times the image is collective: a blurred sense of green shirts outracing the opposition up and down the court, stealing passes, driving for uncontested lay-ups.

And finally, there on the bench (later in the stands), a balding, pudgy character with a mouthful of cigar to symbolize another victory. This is the man who built the tradition and shaped the Celtics' achievement, Arnold "Red" Auerbach. He is the only coach ever to have led his teams to more than 1,000 NBA victories. In twenty coaching seasons, he built a combined regular-season and playoff winning percentage of .654—by far the best record of any professional coach.

Auerbach made his life's work of a sport whose players are drawn from disparate parts of America—from the crowded, increasingly black streets of our inner cities, and from the flat, all-white small towns of the Midwest. And the men who play the pro game are *stars,* accustomed from boyhood to the psychic pleasure of *standing out.* Auerbach's team suited up its fair share of egos, but it always seemed to hang together, winning at crucial moments over and over again. Red called himself a "dictator," and yet the men who were graduated from the team remained strong individuals. They acknowledged a great debt to Auerbach's philosophy, but many adopted radically different styles of coaching and life after leaving the team. Whatever his methods, Auerbach was able to harness the talents of smart, assertive ballplayers without becoming the object of a cult of worshipers.

All this was done in an atmosphere of public indifference, and continuous financial uncertainty. The dynasty teams were forced to compete with their own near-empty treasury and other teams at the same time. To understand the shabby environs of Boston Garden and what was built there, we must first look back at the unpromising beginnings of the team.

2

Beginnings and Tribulations

Along with the green-and-white NBA championship banners hanging from the rafters of Boston Garden, there are two flags decorated only with numbers. Each of the ten numbers identifies someone who helped build the championship tradition: 6 was Russell, of course; 14 was Cousy; 21 was Sharman. But there is one number that was never worn by a Celtic player: the number 1. It was raised to the Garden rafters in the fall of 1964, to honor the memory of the man who founded the Boston Celtics, who bled for the team and lost a fortune trying to keep it together. His devotion to the team may well have hastened his death. The man was Walter Brown.

In an age when owning a professional team has become a millionaire's ego trip or an accountant's tax gimmick, the reputation of Walter Brown defies belief. After his first year, Red Auerbach never had a contract with the man who paid his salary; he had a handshake. Players who today might bring a battery of lawyers and agents to negotiate their con-

tracts trusted Brown implicitly; Frank Ramsey, who became
a highly successful businessman in Kentucky after his playing days were over, used to send his contract in signed, and
tell Brown to fill in the amount he thought was fair. These
seem like episodes from boyhood sports books, those roman-
tic invocations of fair play and honor among comrades, but
they are true.

It is also probably true that without Walter Brown there
would not have been a National Basketball Association. It is
certainly a fact that without him there would not have been
a Boston Celtics franchise, at least not after 1950. He was a
man whose position and wealth was secure—and who risked
all of it to build a basketball team and to keep it going. If
there is a darker side to Walter Brown, if there are secrets
about his professional life, they have never been told, or even
hinted at, more than a decade after his death. He appears to
have been a man whose word was his bond. The impulse that
led him to join in the founding of the Basketball Association
of America was financial: he had an arena to fill, and professional basketball was a way to fill it. But the impulse that led
him to mortgage his home and spend hundreds of thousands
of dollars to keep the Celtics going was something else. He
had made a commitment, and he was going to keep it.

Walter Brown was born in 1905 in Boston, and grew up on
a farm in Hopkinton, Massachusetts. He was the eldest child
of George V. Brown, a prominent figure in the Boston sports
community and, beginning in 1920, general manager of the
Boston Arena, at the time the principal indoor sports arena
in the city. In 1929, New York's Madison Square Garden
built the Boston Garden as a competitor to the Arena. But
five years later, in the depths of the Depression, the Arena
Corporation bought the Garden, and George Brown took
over the newer hall. Walter's father had a genius for promo-
tion; among other things, he was the founder of the Boston
Marathon.

Young Walter received a formal education (Boston Latin School, Hopkinton High, Exeter), but the Arena and the Garden were his playgrounds and his obsessions. He held several jobs in Boston (messenger boy for the Old Colony Trust Company, an insurance broker), but he could not stay away from the indoor halls his father ran. He worked as a ticket-taker, a carpenter, a painter and electrician; he wrote and edited programs, and got his feet wet—or cold—in the promotional business by staging amateur hockey contests. In the early 1930's, he took American amateur hockey teams through Europe, helping to introduce that sport to the continent. In 1933, Brown's American Rangers beat a Toronto team in Prague, the first time a Canadian team had ever lost in world amateur competition. In 1934, George Brown named his son assistant manager of the Garden.

When George Brown died in 1939, thirty-three-year-old Walter became general manager of the Garden-Arena Corporation; two years later, he was named president, a post which he held until his death. He was also president of the Boston Bruins hockey team, president of the Boston Athletic Association, and a vice-president and treasurer of the Ice Capades, which arena managers around the country scheduled to fill open dates. He was a tummeler as well, a promoter who brought Sonja Henie to New York and Boston, who staged boxing matches, a Silver Skates derby, a "swing vs. straight" dance contest that set the all-time Boston Garden attendance record. He even staged an indoor ski-jumping contest, and by World War II (in which he served as a lieutenant colonel) he had increased the nights the Garden was in use from 110 a year to 165.

But in 1945 Brown realized the necessity for something more. "I felt we needed something to add dates to the Garden," he said. "We had a building which cost about a million dollars a year to run, and was being used less than half the nights of the year. Taxes and assessments were spiraling, and ten different unions were annually negotiating for increased contracts." So Brown contacted other owners and managers of arenas in New York, Philadelphia, Chicago and other cities, and suggested a new source of potential revenue: professional basketball.

The dimensions of the risk Walter Brown was suggesting must be explained in some detail. Ever since 1898, with the founding of the National Basketball League, pro ball had been a sputtering, unsuccessful venture. That original National League, comprised of teams from cities in Pennsylvania, New Jersey and New York, lasted little more than a decade. Mostly regional leagues, ill-paying and disorganized, they were born and buried with amazing speed. The most ambitious of the early leagues, the American League, was established in 1926, but its nucleus was dead by 1929, when the Original Celtics (so-called to distinguish them from an earlier team known simply as the Celtics) proved too strong for the league. Playing out of New York, the Original Celtics had such early stars as Joe Lapchick, Nat Holman and Dutch Dehnert. They began as a popular touring team and were forced to enter the American League after being blacklisted by the arena owners who controlled the other teams. So they joined—and proceeded to demolish their opponents and eliminate any competitive excitement. Ultimately, the team was broken up, and shortly afterward the league died; although it resumed operation in 1933, it never regained status as a major league. By 1945, the only professional circuit functioning with any sense of organization was the Midwest-based National Basketball League, with such teams as Fort Wayne, Oshkosh, Sheboygan and Indianapolis.

Given this unencouraging history, it was not surprising that Brown met some resistance from the arena owners he wanted to join with him. Arthur Wirtz, who ran the Chicago Stadium and hockey's Chicago Black Hawks, agreed to come in only if Maurice Podoloff, then president of the American

Hockey League, was picked as president of the new league. Wirtz was also involved with NHL teams in Detroit and New York, and could help organize teams in those cities. Podoloff got the job, and the Basketball Association of America was born at New York's Commodore Hotel on June 9, 1946. The Garden-Arena Corporation created the Boston Celtics, and Walter Brown put himself in charge of the club.

Neither the old NBL nor the new BAA were smooth-running or prosperous in those early seasons. Bob Brannum, who later played with the Celtics, was a member of the Sheboygan Redskins from 1948 to 1950, the last season of the NBL and the first of the new league created by the merger of the NBL and the BAA.

"I was drafted by Sheboygan with another year of eligibility left at Michigan State," he recalled. "I was married at the time, working in an Oldsmobile factory making a dollar fifty an hour. So I signed with Sheboygan for the fabulous sum of six thousand, five hundred; what I actually got was seven-fifty in cash, which was more money than I'd ever seen in my life, and five thousand, five hundred for the year.

"We would travel in automobiles, De Soto Suburbans, which were long cars where the back was open for luggage space. There would be six guys in one car, and five in another. We would play thirteen games in fourteen nights. Leaving Sheboygan for a road trip, we'd play in New York, Providence, Wilkes-Barre, Scranton, Terre Haute, Kansas City and Denver, then end up in Cheyenne, Wyoming. I remember to this day that after playing in Detroit we'd bust our asses till we got to Cadillac, Canada, where the hotel had ropes for fire escapes, and get up at dawn for Syracuse. We used to play rummy games, continually, for fifty cents. But the guy who won had to drive, while the other four could keep playing cards. You'd spend two or three bucks trying lose, so you wouldn't have to drive the damn car."

If Brown had given his fellow arena owners a hard task in

making money out of professional basketball, he had given himself an even harder one in trying to make the sport pay in the city of Boston. Boston is urban America's anchor in New England. Its climate is cold; its geography proximite to Canada, from which the region draws a good number of its inhabitants. And, by climate and populace, it is a city with one dominant winter sport: hockey. For a New Yorker, a mid-winter walk through a working-class neighborhood in Boston causes a kind of culture shock. Where New York kids would clear the snow away from a patch of playground asphalt for a game of one-on-one, Bostonians are skating on a patch of ice along a street, battling with taped-up hockey sticks. When Walter Brown launched the Celtics, he was flying in the face of a formidable cultural barrier. So lacking was the basketball tradition in Boston that the high schools had dropped the sport in the 1920's and had not taken it up again until after the Second World War, which meant that an entire generation of potential basketball fans was all but lost to the Celtics.

Even a successful debut by the Celtics would have had trouble gaining recognition in Boston. Howie McHugh, who joined Walter Brown in 1946 as the Celtics' public relations man and who has been there ever since, remembers, "The Boston *Post* wouldn't carry our box score—it meant they would have had to cover the other teams, and they didn't want to bother." But the new Celtics did not have a successful debut. In fact, in their first four years, they won 89 games and lost 151.

The problem started with the coach. Brown had gone looking for a regionally popular figure to give the new team local credibility and had hired Frank Keaney, whose University of Rhode Island team had nearly won the NIT championship in 1946. But in August, just before the start of the first BAA season, Keaney withdrew from the job because of poor health. Brown then hired John "Honey" Russell, who had been a star player in the late 1920's and a leading college coach at Seton Hall, guiding the team to forty-four straight wins from 1939 to 1941. "He was too late in seeking players," Brown recalled later, "and he never dreamed the league would be as fast as it was." Russell had recruited old-time ball players like Ed Sadowski, Mike Wallace and Tony Kappen, who could not keep up with the younger, faster style of play—particularly the brand played by the Washington Capitals, coached by a thirty-year-old New York public school product named Arnold Auerbach.

The Celtics hit last place in 1946–47. Only the breathtaking 6-42 record of Providence kept them out of last place in 1947–48, despite a 20-28 record. The one Bostonian to rank anywhere among the league leaders was Jim Seminoff, sixth in the league in assists. By this time, the Celtics had already lost $250,000 and the Garden was seriously thinking of forgetting the whole idea. Howie McHugh recalls their pessimism. "I remember telling Walter Brown, 'Jeez, you gotta get rid of this thing.' Brown said, 'I can't. I helped start this league, I gotta stick with it.' I know he started selling a lot of his own stock to cover the team's losses."

After two years, Honey Russell gave up the coaching job, and Brown hit on a way to keep the Garden from abandoning the Celtics. Doggie Julian, the coach at Holy Cross who had led his team to the NCAA championship in 1947, had helped spark new basketball interest in New England. When his 1947–48 team (which included a young player named Bob Cousy) played in Boston, the Garden was packed. Ned Irish, the head of New York's Madison Square Garden, told Brown that Julian might be available, and Brown signed the popular coach, hoping to improve attendance.

It didn't work. Boston finished ahead of Providence in 1948–49, but when the Steamrollers rolled out of the league the next year, the Celtics were back in the cellar. In neither year did they make the playoffs. Julian quit, and so did the

Garden. By then, they had dropped some $460,000 on the team, and were finished with the white elephant. Brown, still feeling the obligation to preserve a charter team of a league he helped to found, offered to buy the team. The Garden said yes, but only if he could find a partner.

Brown went to Lou Pieri, who owned the Rhode Island Auditorium in Providence, and whose previous experience in professional basketball was the Steamrollers, who had cost him some $200,000 in three years. Brown raised his dilemma with Pieri: Where could he find a man willing to invest in a money-losing fifth-rate ball team? Right here, Pieri said. If . . .

The "if" turned out to be a new coach. A coach who had proven he could win.

The coach was Red Auerbach.

•

Arnold "Red" Auerbach was thirty-three years old. And it was clear he could win as a basketball coach. Three years earlier, his Washington Caps had dominated the new BAA, winning forty-nine games and losing only eleven. In the next two years, the Caps stayed near the top of their division. In 1949–50, with much less success, Auerbach coached the Tri-Cities Hawks, a former NBL team in the newly merged National Basketball Association. But the team was hardly promising, and it seemed likely that no coach could have done much better.

The reports on Auerbach weren't altogether favorable, however. For one thing, his teams had usually done well in the regular season but folded in the playoffs. The first-year Caps had lost in the first round to Chicago. The second year, they lost even before the first official round—in a series to break a tie in the season standings. Only in 1948–49 had they gotten to the finals, and then they lost to the Minneapolis Lakers in six games.

Another of Auerbach's apparent problems was getting along with his employers. He asked Washington owner Bob Uline for a multi-year contract after his third season; when Uline refused, Auerbach resigned. His stay in the Tri-Cities had been brief and unhappy; he resigned in mid-season when the Hawks' owner traded a player without consulting him. Clearly, Auerbach didn't tolerate interference.

His tolerance for referees and fans was even less. Bob Brannum remembers the first time he met Auerbach: "It happened in 1949, 1950. I was playing for the Sheboygan Redskins, and Red was coaching at Tri-Cities. It was the year the old National league was merged into the BAA. There was a rivalry between Sheboygan and Tri-Cities you wouldn't believe. And in those days in the NBA, you *won* on your home court. Red used to get thrown out of the games a lot, and he'd go up the balcony and coach from there. The fans loved to yell and scream at him. There was an old man, maybe sixty years old, who was our biggest fan, and he hated Red, *hated* him. One night, Red went racing down the court on a bad call, and this little old bald-headed man runs up to him and belts him with a program, right on top of the head. Red turns around and starts hitting him, and I grabbed Red and held him off. A second later, a cop grabs him and this old man wants him arrested for assault and battery. I talked the cop out of it."

Whatever his reasons, Lou Pieri insisted on this brash young man as the new Celtic coach. Walter Brown needed Pieri's support, so he agreed. The fans and sportswriters in Boston were somewhat restrained in their reaction, and soon they had a reason to doubt the new coach's good sense.

Auerbach's real introduction to Boston was the notorious press conference whose ironies were to sharpen for the next fifteen years. When Auerbach arrived in Boston, the local basketball hero was guard Bob Cousy, who had broken the all-time scoring record at Holy Cross and dazzled fans with his shooting, passing and ball-handling antics. But Auerbach's prejudices ran heavily against the individualist. And Cousy was only six-foot-one. Auerbach needed a big man to dominate the boards and trigger the break, and Cousy didn't fit the description.

At the press conference, the Boston writers asked Auerbach if he was planning to exercise his territorial draft rights over Cousy. Auerbach looked over at Walter Brown and uttered one of the better lines Boston had heard since Paul Revere announced the arrival of the Redcoats. "Am I supposed to win," he asked, "or am I supposed to impress the local yokels?"

The Celtics did not draft Cousy, and Auerbach had shown in his first Boston encounter a trait that would remain through all his years with the team: he was more interested in winning ball games than in winning the hearts and minds of the Boston fans.

Red Auerbach was born in 1917 in the Williamsburg section of Brooklyn. He went to the nonexclusive P.S. 122, then to Eastern District High School, where he played basketball and made the second team of the all-Brooklyn high school squad. "A lot of my players laugh at this," he says, "until I tell them Brooklyn probably had more kids in it than their states did."

When Auerbach went looking for a college, the competition was fierce. "In those days," he remembers, "NYU used to have tryouts for scholarships. They would have a hundred ball players come out looking for two or three scholarships. So I went up to NYU and did pretty well at the tryout, but they told me, 'You gotta go to the School of Commerce.' I said, 'Heck, I want to be a phys. ed. teacher, I don't want any part of that.' So before they could say no, or whatever, I told them I wasn't interested. Then Nat Holman wanted me to go to City College, where he coached, and I couldn't get in. I was President of Eastern District and I had an 87 average, but in those days you needed a 93. So Holman wanted to put me in night schools for six months and have me transferred over, but I didn't go for that. So I went instead to Seth Low Junior College [in New York], where I had a partial scholarship. Isaac Asimov, the science-fiction writer, was one of my classmates. He was a helluva guy.

"We had a helluva ball club. We only had a hundred and seventy-five students. I remember, we played St. John's University—the varsity—and they beat us by thirteen points, but with two minutes to go there was only a three-point difference. We played Brooklyn College and split with them, we played St. Francis, and we used to beat the hell out of teams like Seton Hall, Brooklyn Poly, St. Peters, all those teams. We beat 'em with the break."

The break was taught them by their coach, Gordon Ritings, a protégé of Bill Reinhart, who was then the coach at George Washington University. After two years at Seth Low, Auerbach transferred to GW and played under Reinhart himself. Ever after, he spoke of his college coach with awe. "The man who taught me this game was Bill Reinhart at George Washington," he said years later. "He is probably the greatest brain in the history of basketball. He used the fast break in the 1930's, the same fast break we installed with the Caps in Washington, the very same fast break I took to the Boston Celtics. And the Celtics still use it today. Reinhart was twenty years ahead of his time."

Even as a college player, however, Auerbach had a critical eye. "He was a strong disciplinarian, but not strong enough," he said of Reinhart. "He was too nice a guy." Auerbach would also learn from his mentor's mistakes.

At George Washington, Red averaged 10.6 points a game, good enough to make him the leading scorer in the D.C. metropolitan area. After graduation, he coached high school and—believe it or not—refereed on the side. ("That's one of the reasons I never played pro ball," he said. "I was making more money as a referee.")

He also learned something from his work as a recreation

aide in Washington at the National Training School for Boys, a reform school. As he tells the story in his book, *Winning the Hard Way,* one sixteen-year-old caught in a stolen car swore to Auerbach that he was just riding around with a friend. When Auerbach inquired about the case, he found that the young innocent had a long record of theft, moonshine running, and white slavery. One day when Auerbach was running a session, the boys suddenly got interested and peppered him with questions about the game. Auerbach began answering enthusiastically. Then he looked around and saw another group of kids bending back a heavy metal window guard in an effort to escape. "So I learned very early that you had to look a little deeper, no matter who you were dealing with," Auerbach concluded. "I learned that con men come in all ages, all sizes."

After coaching Navy teams successfully during World War II, the twenty-nine-year-old Auerbach walked into the office of Bob Uline, owner of the Washington Capitals in the new BAA, and convinced him he was the man to build a new ball club. Impressed either by Auerbach's confidence or by his record, Uline gave him the job, and Red went about building a basketball team.

Auerbach had a theory: recruit from as wide a geographic area as possible to take advantage of the distinct skills and attributes of players. "In those days," he recalls, "you'd get your best ball handlers from New York, rebounders from the West and Midwest, shooters from the West, and one-hand jump shooters from the South." He built a team and designed a style that would find its full flower in Boston, with the Celtics.

He applied Reinhart's basic theory that you win in basketball by outrunning the other team. He moved his tallest player, John Mahnken, into the corner, trying to draw away the opposing center from the middle, leaving it free for a big guard to bring a smaller man down near the basket and shoot

over him. (This is still one of the Celtics' favorite scoring
tactics.) He built plays around screens, trying to free a reliable shooter to take a jump shot relatively unhampered by
the defense. (Five years later, he would find the man who
could take full advantage of this maneuver—Bill Sharman.)
And he was already beginning to stress depth, boasting that
none of his players were among the top ten in scoring. After
a good first year and a mediocre second one, the Caps went
all the way to the playoff finals in 1949.

But there were rumors that Fred Scolari, the Caps' ball-
handling guard, wanted the coaching job for himself, so
Auerbach demanded a long-term contract. His demand was
turned down, and he resigned. Under player-coach Scolari,
the team had their first losing season in 1949–50, and on
January 9, 1951, they disbanded.

Auerbach signed up as coach of the Tri-Cities Black-
hawks. When he resigned in mid-season, he was married,
with a family and without a job. Then came the offer from
Boston.

After his ill-advised first press conference, Auerbach settled down and began to build a team. Charlie Share, whom
he drafted instead of Cousy, never amounted to much. But
Cousy himself arrived, his name being literally picked out of
a hat. Bill Sharman followed, dissuaded from a baseball
career. Then, in 1953, Auerbach took three starters from a
great University of Kentucky team in three successive
rounds of the draft—Frank Ramsey, Cliff Hagan and Lou
Tsiriopoulous. Kentucky had been suspended from all inter-
collegiate play during the 1952–53 season, and the rest of the
NBA teams ignored the players since they had been given an
extra year of eligibility. Auerbach read the rules more carefully and interpreted them literally. The determining factor,
he argued, was whether the players' entering class had graduated. The league officials immediately clarified the rule for

future drafts, but they had to let Auerbach have his Kentuckians.

Each season, the Celtics won more games than they lost and qualified for the playoffs. Basketball fans began to appreciate the team's skills, and Auerbach received increasing attention—for his excitable nature on the court if not for his coaching talent. The playoffs, however, were a different story. The Celtics were eliminated each year, losing to New York the first three seasons, to Dolph Schayes's Syracuse Nationals the next three.

Even misfortune in the playoffs never caused Auerbach to waver. He followed his theory and kept a tight grip on his players. While he waited for the man or men who would complete the team, he developed those parts of the game that would mark his style.

"Red always wanted press, press, pressure defense, to force the other teams out of their styles," Bob Brannum recalls. "At times, we'd be down by nine points with two minutes to go, and we'd win some of those games because of the press. He was realistic enough to know he didn't have the greatest talent in the world, but he never doubted himself. Never. Never. Did you ever hear of anyone who ever said he did? Never.

"He always demanded you come into camp a certain weight. A couple of times when people didn't, Red raised hell. Because he always believed you could get off to a quick start if you were in shape while the other guys were working themselves up after the season had started.

"And he was always the boss. Never any question about that. He'd say, 'I may not always be right, but I am never wrong.' "

Auerbach imposed his own prejudices on his players without question. You could drink beer, a quart of it at a time, but wine, liquor, or drinks that looked like liquor, meant a fine—because he didn't want to bother checking a suspicious glass. His force of will was so great that Bob Brannum once met his ex-coach at a dinner, *nine years* after he had put away his Celtic uniform for the last time, and hid a glass of Scotch he was drinking. A player could stuff himself with ham and eggs for breakfast—but a stack of pancakes would cost him $25.

Auerbach could sum up a basketball precept with simple, untechnical language that would cut through the pretensions of a dozen theorists. "You've got a basketball," he once said. "It's round. The floor's even. If you bounce it, it's going to come straight up. You don't have to watch it. One of the most important things in basketball is the position of the head. The game is *not* played down there. It's played up here."

He would take ideas from wherever he found them. His essential philosophy—the fast break—is drawn directly from the thinking of his hero, Bill Reinhart. The Boston dress code, never written down but always followed by the players, who wore jackets with ties or turtlenecks, came from a discussion with Phil Rizzuto, who told Auerbach how Yankee manager Joe McCarthy used it to impress on his players the special pride of being a Yankee.

He would take on anyone to fight for his team. If a referee was calling fouls against the Celtics, he would protest until he was thrown out of the game as a deliberate emotional spark to his players. (In his coaching years, he was assessed a record $18,000 in fines.) He would fight for every psychological edge; it was said that he carried a portable ten-foot pole with him to measure the height of the rims in other arenas.

His finest words of praise on behalf of a player was that the man was willing to "pay the price" for his success—by conditioning, practice and self-sacrifice, as in the case of Bill Sharman (and later K.C. Jones and John Havlicek). And Auerbach himself paid a price. For twenty-five years, he lived four hundred miles from his wife and children in Washington, to cut himself off from the distractions that stood between him and his job. "I don't think he would have had the success he had if his family had been underfoot all the time," his wife Dorothy said recently. "I think he's a genius in his own business, and geniuses need a lot of room."

Left alone, he lived like an adolescent who had spent his first years under rigid parental supervision and was suddenly let free with ample funds and no one around. His diet was a nutritionist's nightmare: hot dogs for breakfast, pastrami sandwiches for lunch, soda pop at 9 A.M., cartons full of Chinese food at midnight. He has, he says, never eaten an egg or drunk a cup of coffee in his life, and perhaps he will be proven to have been the Adele Davis of the junk food set; for all of the stress of his life he has never taken a sleeping pill or a tranquilizer (the same cannot be said about those who worked or played for or against him). Yet he had a firm philosophy about food: "I can't eat before a game. It's a plain psychological thing. After you eat, you sit down. What happens? You go to sleep. Who are the most dangerous people? Animals. A hungry tiger. Not a starving tiger, a hungry tiger."

This kind of competitive spirit, or ferocity, was an Auerbach characteristic throughout his career, and especially in those days before Boston had built its dynasty. It was something Auerbach liked to be part of, even when the outbursts were spontaneous rather than planned.

Bob Brannum recalls one incident that was typical of Auerbach: "We were playing Baltimore. They had a player named Paul Hoffman who was like I was. He'd stop anybody driving for the basket. Cousy went to the basket a couple of times, and Hoffman really racked him up. So I said to Cousy, 'Bring him through.' And when he came through, I whacked him. The next day, the same thing is happening. He went up for a lay-up and I knocked him into the second row. Hoffman got up, didn't even look at me, and went charging to the bench, screaming at Auerbach, 'You son of a bitch, you *told* him to do that!'' And Auerbach said, 'You're damn right I did!' "

And even though Auerbach had not yet won a title, among his players he already had a reputation for omniscience. "Auerbach seemed to be everywhere at all times," Brannum says. "When I was playing with the Celtics one day, my wife and I went out to dinner with some friends to a night club in Revere. When I got to practice the next day, Red says, 'Went to a night club last night, right? Bottle of liquor on the table, right?'

" 'But Red,' I said, 'I didn't have any.'

" 'I know it,' he said."

By 1955, despite his talent and modicum of success, Auerbach was skating on thin ice. Before the 1954–55 season, Walter Brown had announced that his coach was taking a cut in salary. The mild-mannered Brown said the cut was "my way of saying that I hold him partially responsible for the failure of the team. It was one of the conditions of his returning." One of the Boston writers put the dagger in even deeper. Auerbach, he said, was "the most overrated coach in the league."

After another loss to Syracuse in the 1956 playoffs, Auerbach studied the draft choices available to him. One who was not readily available was Bill Russell, the six-foot-nine center for the University of San Francisco. It was time for Auerbach to make his move, and he did so with characteristic boldness. Trading away two of the mainstays of his team, Easy Ed Macauley and Cliff Hagan, he got the draft choice that assured Russell for Boston. Then, using his territorial pick, he took a big forward from Holy Cross, a man named Tom Heinsohn.

With that 1956 draft, the days of frustration were over. Auerbach had built a team that brought an NBA title to

Boston—and that kept it there virtually without interruption for the next thirteen years. Yet his most impressive achievement lay not so much in the development of, and faith in, a theory. It was his selection and motivation of the most remarkable collection of players in basketball history, each of them with a specific talent to bring to the making of a champion. It is their stories—both as players and as men—that form the important threads of the Celtic dynasty.

Part Two
Playing

3

Bob Cousy:
The Perfectionist

Throughout the postwar years, there were two great popular professional sports in Boston: hockey and baseball. And for fifteen of those years, first as a collegian and then as a pro, there was one totally popular sports hero in that town: Bob Cousy, a basketball player. It was as if Liberace had conquered a rock festival, or Yassir Arafat had brought the house down at Hadassah. Yet the fact is that only Ted Williams rivaled Cousy as the most popular local athlete of his day, and even so, there was always a hard core of Williams detractors. Williams was booed in Boston until he announced his retirement; Cousy received nothing but cheers, and ultimately tears, of affection.

As an All-American at Holy Cross, and then as a perennial All-Star with the Celtics, Cousy was the first to make Boston's sports fans aware that basketball was an exciting, entertaining contest. Given the shaky condition of the Celtics, it is not too much to say that without him the franchise might never have survived to become a title-winning team.

Cousy was responsible for more exciting moments in the history of the National Basketball Association than any other player. His 50-point performance in a four-overtime win against Syracuse in the 1953 playoff—in which he hit on 30 of 32 free throws and scored 12 points in the last five-minute overtime—still stands as one of the great moments in the team's history.

From his rookie year until the year he retired, he was on every NBA All-Star team; he was the Celtics' top playmaker for all of those years, and for eight years in a row he also led the league. And while the Celtics were building their teams into contention, he led the club in scoring as well—for four consecutive years.

But it was his style as much as his records that made Cousy so appealing to the fans. He was a product of the New York playgrounds (although he came out of the Long Island high schools), and he had the classic playground qualities: great speed, spectacular deception, and the ability to change direction while retaining total control of the ball. In his ability to spot the open man, to move the ball away from the opposition, and to combine playmaking and scoring strengths, Cousy was the model for later players like Nate "Tiny" Archibald (who was coached by Cousy in his early pro years). When Auerbach lists the players who shaped the game, he includes the six-one Cousy for "proving that there was room for the small man in pro ball."

Like dozens of others, Cousy found in basketball a path from poverty to fame and fortune. He thrived on competition and was willing to endure enormous physical and emotional pain because of it. He was a hungry ballplayer, driven by a fierce need to prove himself, a force which calls "the killer instinct." Years later, he came to question the drive that sends a man out to win at any cost, but he remained convinced that without it, neither his success—nor that of the Celtics—would ever have happened. He became, in a sense, an Auerbach with another dimension: as motivated, as driven, as the guru himself, but able to see the athletic ethic from a different perspective. Bound up as he was in the competitive world, he differed from his coach and many of his contemporaries in that he recognized the darker side of the endless struggle for victory.

Bob Cousy was born in 1928 in a tenement section of Manhattan to parents of French descent (whence comes his lifelong speech quirk of mixing his *r*'s and *w*'s). He was conscious from childhood of his family's lack of money; he rooted for the Yankees because "they were always a winner, and I liked a winner." He began to play basketball when he was thirteen, after his parents moved to St. Albans, Queens, a suburban area of New York City. In high school, he began to gain recognition, and he spent his summers playing at resorts in the Catskill Mountains, with such future stars as George Mikan, Ed Macauley and Dolph Schayes.

Cousy's college career was almost over before it started. Accepting a scholarship to Holy Cross, he clashed with coach "Doggie" Julian, and grew so restive that he went to see St. John's coach Joe Lapchick, hoping to transfer. Lapchick advised him to stay at Holy Cross. But the friction continued: in one game, he was benched for an entire half; when Julian ordered him to go into the game in the last thirty seconds, he refused. Before Cousy's junior year, however, Julian left to take over the Celtics, and Buster Sheary became the Holy Cross coach.

It was in his junior year that Cousy first demonstrated his capacity to bring a basketball crowd to its feet. In a close game against Loyola, he was driving to his right when an opponent stepped in front of him and shut off his path to the basket. Without thinking about it, Cousy bounced the ball behind his back, picked up the dribble with his left hand, and scored with a left-handed hook. The crowd loved it, and

Cousy had discovered a weapon, and a style, that was to become his trademark.

In his last two years at Holy Cross, Cousy won a large share of publicity—unusual for a New England community like Worcester, forty miles west of Boston. In 1949, he broke the all-time Holy Cross scoring record with a 26-point effort against Dartmouth. In the first four games of his senior season, he scored 90 points in ninety-three minutes, while his teammates said Cousy was passing the ball too much. And in December, before the second biggest college crowd in the history of the Cleveland Arena, Cousy scored 24 points and controlled the ball brilliantly in a 71–70 overtime victory against Bowling Green—and he did it with his left leg wrapped in tape from knee to ankle. Cousy had tied the game with five seconds to go on a forty-foot shot.

In the last ninety seconds of a game against Kansas University in his senior year, Cousy stole a pass, sunk a lay-up, stole the in-bounds pass, scored another lay-up, and ran out the clock, sinking two free throws in a 57–53 victory. The Kansas coach, the venerable Phog Allen, said, "I see it, but I don't believe it." And an NCAA official said after that performance, "I've seen all the college stars of this game, but Cousy is far ahead of anyone. He is so far out of this basketball world that it's hard to compare him to anyone."

Nonetheless, Auerbach refused to use the Celtics' territorial draft to take Cousy, preferring to try for a bigger man. But Cousy seemed fated to end up in Boston. He was drafted by the Tri-Cities Hawks (Auerbach's former unhappy home) and signed for $9,000—then a high figure. But the Hawks soon found themselves owing a player to the Chicago Stags, and they sent Cousy. There was still more funny business to come. The Stags went out of business before the 1950–51 season. Cousy wound up in a player pool which included two proven stars, Max Zaslofsky and Andy Phillip. Three teams had claims on the Stags—Boston, New York and Philadelphia—and all three wanted Zaslofsky. The three names were placed in a hat, and the owners drew to decide the matter. Walter Brown chose last and (according to judgments at the moment) worst: he got Bob Cousy for the Celtics.

Brown was crestfallen. "I thought I got stung," he said later. "I'd had a bellyful of hometown heroes. We picked up half of that great 1947 Holy Cross team, including George Kaftan, Joe Mullaney and Dermie O'Connell. We tried Tony Lavelli from Yale [who used to entertain the fans with his accordion at half time] and Ed Leede from Dartmouth, and none of them made the grade. Why should I think Cousy would be any different?"

Although in Cousy's and Auerbach's first year at Boston the Celtics had their first winning season, there was a persistent sense of conflict between the two. Auerbach was, after all, a coach to whom flamboyance and individualism were highly suspect. And Cousy was a highly flamboyant, individualistic player. More important, the other Celtics had trouble adjusting to the unexpected nature of Cousy's moves. Several of his teammates tell the same story: the Celtics breaking downcourt, Cousy controlling the ball, when suddenly an unsuspecting player is hit in the head or shoulder by an unexpected pass.

It was Auerbach's thesis that "in pro ball, the players are highly coordinated, well-conditioned men; so it stands to reason that 90 percent of the times a pass is dropped, it's the passer's fault." Looking back, Auerbach says of Cousy's early years, "He was like atomic energy that couldn't be controlled. He threw the ball all over the place, hitting his own guys on the back of the head. He had to learn to adjust himself to each of his teammates . . . There's no sense fooling the opposition if you're fooling your own men, too."

Auerbach tried to intimidate Cousy with his gruff, overbearing manner. Spotting him coming into a New York hotel one night, Auerbach shouted across the lobby, "Where the hell have you been?" "None of your business," Cousy boomed right back. "He never tried that again," Cousy recalls.

Midway through the 1953 season, Auerbach publicly criticized Cousy, saying that he was "trying too much of that behind-the-back razzle-dazzle. The other clubs are wise to us, and they jammed up the middle." Stung by the criticism, and by the public comments of Walter Brown, who compared his stars' high salaries with their lack of success, Cousy went on a local radio show and suggested it might be time for a trade. That cooled off the tempestuous Brown, and in time Auerbach came to appreciate that Cousy's talents actually fit in perfectly with his own essential basketball theory.

The fast break, after all, depends on a skilled ball handler who can instinctively size up the best scoring opportunity on the run. When a team is streaking downcourt, the ball handler cutting down the middle must have the peripheral vision to know where every teammate and opponent is, the basketball sense to know what opportunity is likely to open up, and the ability to put the ball where the opportunity is. Cousy's instincts, his ability to dribble and pass, and his capacity to shoot if an opponent attempted to sag off him to block a passing lane, made him an ideal component of a fast-break system.

Sometimes, Cousy's ball handling was all but hypnotic. Bill Sharman recalls a game against New York in which Cousy twice flipped the ball behind his back to Sharman, baffling the Knicks' Richie Guerin. The third time Cousy brought the ball downcourt, Guerin jumped out to block the pass. Cousy faked the pass, kept the ball, and went in for an uncontested lay-up. "Someday," a referee said, "somebody's going to tell me that Cousy has just swallowed the ball, and I'm simply going to go over to the bench and get a new one."

If there was any one game that brought his magic to the attention of a national basketball audience, it was Cousy's performance in the 1954 East-West All-Star game, a contest New York *Times* writer Arthur Daley called "the best basketball game this observer ever saw."

After the West tied the game at the buzzer to force an overtime, Cousy scored 10 points in five minutes, passed the ball several times to open teammates, and killed the clock, dribbling between the best players in the West. The East won, 98–93. The writers, who had already voted the MVP award to Minneapolis' Jim Pollard, called for another vote and gave Cousy the trophy.

Cousy was also a court psychologist. He would deliberately withhold some of his firepower until the second half, leading his opponent to gear himself to a certain level of play. Then suddenly he would increase his own pace in the second half when the game grew close and pull away from the opponent. (In a 1958 game against Syracuse, Boston was 13 points down in the second half; Cousy scored 29 points in that half to give the Celtics a 1-point victory.)

Cousy also knew that his teammates, no matter how much they were a part of the team, wanted chances to score. And so, he recalled later, "when I was working the ball up, I'd try and remember who'd gotten the ball or the basket the last time, and then I'd pass to somebody else. The big men are doing the hard and violent work, and if they're not getting the 'sugar'—those x's in the scorebook after their name—then they're not happy."

Ex-teammate Bob Brannum remembers, "I found out that when I wasn't looking for a pass and he threw it off my nose and out of bounds, I didn't see the ball for a week. I learned that with Cousy if you move and you're looking, you get the ball. If you stand around, you don't get it." In such ways, Cousy motivated his teammates to play harder, to work for the open shot, to hustle.

When Cousy played basketball, it was a matter of total concentration, an act of deeply personal, egotistical pleasure and enormous stress. And it left him totally spent. "I used to drive home from Boston to Worcester after a game," he told me, "especially after a successful game, and I'd have trouble staying awake at the wheel."

Yet he was an athlete who demanded not release from pressure, but its presence, sitting alone in hotel rooms, mentally working up an intense, personal hatred for the man he was to play against in the coming game. "A lot of athletes," he says, "when they get into an agitated state, lose their cool and they can't function. I always looked for that feeling."

All of this is a conventional enough story of an unconventionally gifted athlete. And yet, for all the wealth and fame that came to Cousy because of his basketball skills, he was never content to take the money and run—on or off the court. His thesis in college was on the persecution of minority groups. He was by instinct a sympathizer with the people on the short end of the stick: "If I were young and black," he said recently, "I'd be out there throwing bricks." He founded the NBA Players' Association in 1955, fighting for recognition of the group as the bargaining agent for the players, despite the fact that he was one of the highest-paid players in the league. "I knew," he says, "that I was one of the *only* ones who could start it without risking a career."

He was also willing, long before it became the fashion among some writers and athletes, to make links between the world of big-time athletics and the greater society. When the point-shaving scandals exploded again in 1961, catching up dozens of players in a welter of accusations, Cousy had some tough things to say at a high school athletic award dinner: "I find it very hard," he said, "to make these ballplayers any more criminal than the 'point-shaving' on millions of tax returns and illegal insurance rebates that many try to finagle. This is the society that these players have been brought up in, and to my way of thinking, the players involved are the least guilty of anyone at all involved in creating their environment."

And when he was challenged, he did not back down. There is, he said, "a deplorable breakdown in our moral fiber, such matters as fraudulent income tax returns, cheating of our insurance companies, quiz show scandals, recent exposés of political corruption, and industrial kickbacks. But more to my point is the competitive procurement whereby many of our universities recruit youngsters by under-the-table inducements, which are a clear violation of our amateur code."

Ironically, it was this same complaint that, years later, would drive Cousy out of the college, and then professional, coaching ranks. The sport he had helped to make so popular was to grow so lucrative, and so intensely competitive in the fight for talent, that it was to prove too much even for a competitor like Cousy.

But most revealing was Cousy's own willingness to talk about the emotional consequences of the pressure to win. He has been all his life a battler; even today, he says, "I may start out playing tennis for fun, and end up swinging at my opponent and my partner." Yet by the end of his career he was putting into print the feelings of a man who had spent his life in an intense experience of winning and losing. He wrote of nightmares so real and frightening that, when away from the release of playing basketball, he was driven from his bed and in one case through the screen door of a vacation bungalow into the night woods; nightmares so real that he would have to be tied down to a bed to keep him from injuring himself. He described the physical sensations of pressure: the nerve jumping under his left arm, the tic under his left eye, the signals of the body in a state of emotional stress that all somehow was channeled into excellence when the ball was thrown up for the opening tap.

The steals, the passes, the dribbling, the shooting, the pressure defense, the basketball sense and the crowd-pleasing style of play gave Cousy a stature unmatched by any other first-generation player in the NBA, George Mikan and Bob Pettit included. The vote for the Player of the Decade, 1951–60, wasn't even close—Cousy won by a landslide.

His formal "farewell" appearance at Boston Garden on St. Patrick's Day, 1963, brought an outpouring of sentiment that resembled Lou Gehrig's farewell a quarter of a century earlier. The mayor and the governor appeared. President Kennedy sent a telegram of warm congratulations. Cousy was showered with gifts. He and Auerbach wept in each other's arms as the crowd, tearful themselves, looked on. Then Martha Grady, the cystic fibrosis poster girl, came out to thank Cousy, who had spent years raising funds for the charity. When she threw her arms around him and hugged him, he broke up completely. As he stood at the microphone to read his notes, he repeatedly stopped to try and control the tears. While the Garden silently waited for Cousy to compose himself, a thirty-two-year-old city worker named Joseph Dillon leaned over the balcony and boomed out, "We all love you, Cooz!" When Cousy finally finished, the applause lasted three minutes and twenty seconds.

Throughout his playing days, Cousy had had an outlet for the tension, for his ambivalent attitudes toward the whole enterprise of competition. It was only when he stopped playing, when he entered the world of athletics as a coach, that he found himself unable to carve out a happy middle ground for himself. The same drive that had taken him to the top of his profession, that had made him a demigod, was to drive him out of the profession for the sake of his health and his sanity.

4

Bill Sharman: The Golden Boy

Among sports legends, none is more familiar than that of the Golden Boy, the naturally gifted athlete who is marked for success in boyhood, whose athletic skills make him a hero from early youth. In the legend, the Golden Boy is a dedicated athlete who spends hours improving his already considerable skills, compulsively making the most of himself.

Bill Sharman was such a Golden Boy. And for most of his life, all the dreams came true.

Yet there was a sense of dissatisfaction that seemed to follow Sharman throughout his remarkably successful career; always a suggestion of a better life over the next hill, a potential not quite realized. In Bill Sharman, one can read the reality that the Golden Boy legends somehow seem to leave out—even when the legend comes as close to fulfillment as it has in the career of Bill Sharman.

Like Bob Cousy, Sharman was a fierce competitor. But in other ways he was Cousy's opposite, as different in style and background as is the small town of Porterville, California, from Cousy's New York City. Where Cousy showed off playground skills and thrills, Sharman was a mechanical machine doggedly practicing not in a teeming big-city schoolyard, but in a solitary backyard. He believed in endless repetition, in perfecting skills by beating the untrustworthy impulses of the body and mind into submission. Sharman played basketball, and later taught it, with strict fealty to these principles. His intensity brought grudging respect for his success, but little affection from men he played with or coached. The same ex-Celtics who spoke of him as "the best natural athlete who ever played the game" also described him as selfish. "He would go through a brick wall," one says, "if he could score."

For Auerbach, Sharman—with his compulsiveness and determination to score—was part of the team. Just as Red's ideal team needed a rebounder, a playmaker, a defensive specialist, so it needed one man whose primary job was to put the ball in the basket. Auerbach knew that a key part of winning with a fast-break team was to plan for those times when a team couldn't break. If the defense was set, Auerbach liked to send his players cutting off screens and picks, giving them for a split second an uncontested shot at the basket. While Cousy was a good shooter, his responsibilities as a quarterback and playmaker made it impossible for him to play the role of shooter as well. To fill that spot, Auerbach looked not for a spinning, twisting, one-on-one player who set up his own opportunities, but for a methodical player who could shoot with machine-like reliability, who could convert the opportunity into 2 points as frequently as human fallibility permitted.

The sense of methodical hard work was already a part of Sharman's life when he was six years old. He would shoot baskets in the backyard of his home for hours ar a time— when he wasn't running to improve his conditioning, or playing baseball, his first love. By the time he reached high school, he was realizing the life of the legend: he was captain of the football team, first baseman on the baseball team, a championship tournament tennis player. Porterville was a small town on the edge of California's great central valley, and Bill was the greatest athlete the town had ever produced. He won fifteen letters at Porterville High. Apart from baseball, football and basketball, he was a shot-putter, a javelin-thrower, a hurdler, a weight-lifter and an undefeated boxer. Once, on a single day in 1944, he won the shot put and discus, and ran third in the high hurdles, at a morning track meet; won the San Joacquin Valley tennis tournament in the early afternoon; and later pitched his team to a baseball victory. When he turned eighteen, Sharman graduated from high school, married Ileana Bough, his high school sweetheart, and enlisted in the Navy.

Returning from the service, Sharman attended the University of Southern California, where he limited his athletic competition to baseball, basketball and tennis. He also won very good grades, largely by studying harder and more methodically than his classmates. By this time in his life, Sharman's emphasis on method and regularity was set; there were lists, projects and an attempt to reduce his life to a routine. "I've always been a planner," he says. "I always had a lot of notes in my pocket, even as a kid. I like to plan each day, I like to plan each week, I like to plan ahead to try and make things go as smooth as possible."

By his junior year, Sharman was playing basketball well enough to threaten the Pacific Coast Conference season scoring record of the Stanford immortal Hank Luisetti. In his senior year, he broke the invincible record, scoring 26 points in the last game to accumulate 239 points in conference games. But Sharman did not stay to get his degree at Southern California. The Brooklyn Dodgers had given him a contract and a bonus, and Sharman, already a father, had an occupation to pursue. Before he left, USC held a "Bill Sharman Day." And he became the first basketball player to have his footprints embedded in Phelps Terkel's Perpetual Concrete Hall of Fame.

For five years, beginning while he was still in college, Sharman pursued his dream of playing major league baseball. He played for Pueblo in the Western League, batting .288; Elmira, Fort Worth, St. Paul, always batting in the high .200's, always mixing baseball with school and basketball in the winter, never quite performing up to major league standards.

Sharman entered the NBA in 1950, playing for the hapless Washington Caps. As if to accommodate him, the Caps folded in January, allowing him to get an early start on the baseball season. By that September, he had been brought up to the Brooklyn Dodgers to fill in for outfielders Duke Snider or Carl Furillo once the Dodgers clinched the pennant. But that was the year of the New York Giants' miraculous comeback, and the Dodgers lost. Sharman never got into a game.

Now he had a choice to make: baseball or basketball? When the Caps folded, his basketball talents had become the property of the Fort Wayne Pistons. That seemed to decide the matter; Sharman would head for the Caribbean and play winter baseball rather than play in Fort Wayne. He told Fred Zollner, owner of the Pistons, that he wouldn't be appearing.

At this point, Red Auerbach came on the scene. Bones McKinney, who had played for the Caps from their early days under Auerbach until their final game, told Red that Sharman was a great shooter. Coincidentally, the Pistons owed the Celtics a player on an earlier trade. Auerbach called Fred Zollner and asked for Sharman. Zollner figured he had nothing to lose since Sharman was planning to play winter baseball anyway, so he agreed.

As Sharman tells it, when Auerbach called and asked him to come to Boston, he demanded so much money—$12,000

—that the Celtics would have to turn him down. To his surprise, they met his excessive price and he finally decided to join, becoming with Bob Cousy one of the great backcourt combinations in basketball history.

In a decade with the Boston Celtics, Sharman established himself as one of the greatest shooters ever to play the game. "The best shooter from the backcourt ever," Auerbach called him. In his professional career, Sharman averaged .423 on floor shooting, taking his shots almost exclusively from the twenty-foot perimeter. From 1955 to 1959, he was Boston's leading scorer, averaging almost 21 points a game in those four seasons.

The proper measure of his shooting, however, and an impressive proof of a theory—that of hard, repetitive practice —came in Sharman's free-throw shooting. Here, where the sole test is accuracy, concentration and will, Sharman developed into the best foul shooter ever. For every one of his ten years with the Celtics, he led the club in shooting from the foul line; for seven of those years, he led the league. His .932 percentage in the 1958–59 season still stands as the best record ever. He set a record (still unbroken) of fifty-six straight free throws in the playoffs, and another (broken in 1975 by Calvin Murphy) of fifty-five straight in regular-season competition. Free-throw shooting is, after all, a pure test of concentration and body mechanics, and Sharman was the unequaled master of training the body to repeat the motions of an athletic skill almost at will.

Sharman's job was to shoot. He took some abuse for his willingness to score, but he was not the gunner his reputation suggests. Both Cousy and Heinsohn averaged more shots per season than did Sharman.

But putting the ball in the basket was his primary job. "To tell me that I should pass off when I have a shot," he observed, "is like telling Cousy he should let somebody else get the assists, or telling Russell that he should give somebody else a chance to take the rebounds." And, in fact, the Celtic offense was set up to take advantage of the contrasting skills of Cousy and Sharman. Cousy had the capacity to make things happen on the court; to draw defenders away toward himself on a drive or toward a pass that was never thrown. Sharman had the capacity to turn such an opportunity into a score; he simply knew better than anyone else how to shoot a basketball. Thus, on a fast break, Cousy was the ball handler, moving down the middle of the court looking for a forward along the sidelines, and Sharman was the trailer. If the forwards were covered, and if Cousy did not have a good open shot from the foul line, his other option was to flip the ball over his shoulder to Sharman. And, if the fast break was shut down, it was Sharman who was best equipped to use the momentary freedom given a shooter by a screen or a pick.

Part of Sharman's skill came from his physical equipment. Bud Palmer, who played for the New York Knickerbockers before becoming a sports announcer, said that "one of Bill's greatest assets is his hands. He seems to caress the ball every time he handles it. Bill also has great fingertip control, which, in the act of shooting, allows him to retain control of the ball at a point where most players have already let it go. This is known as 'full extension.' Those extra seconds Bill controls the ball give him a better line to the basket. He almost seems to hate to let go of the ball, and when he does, he has perfect follow-through . . . Sharman has a very soft shot, too. It seems to hit the rim with the impact of a snowflake."

As his amateur athletic career shows, Sharman had a kind of "pure" natural athletic ability that would have made him a fine athlete regardless of his mental attitude; he apparently had the same gift from fate as has John Havlicek: a tireless body. But Sharman's sense of compulsion extended to his body. He was and is an indefatigable exerciser, who would come into training camp in better shape than anyone else, after weeks of long-distance running. During one off-season, on a motoring trip with his family, Sharman got out of the car during a fill-up and decided to run ahead along the highway for exercise. His wife drove after him, then assumed she had missed him and doubled back along the highway; in fact, Sharman had simply run further than she could have imagined.

Sharman's physical equipment, however, is only part of the explanation for his shooting. Many athletes believe that their skills are instinctive, a matter of feel and rhythm. They can no more explain or describe what they do in the midst of competition than they can "explain" how they breathe. But the methodical, compulsive Sharman treated shooting the way a Swiss jeweler treats a watch: by breaking it down part by part and working on it, over and over and over.

When Sharman came into professional basketball, the conventional wisdom was to aim for the front rim of the basket; hoping to put the ball just over the rim. No, said Sharman. Aim for the *back* rim. Why? First, if you shoot long, there's always the chance the backboard will make up for your mistake. Second, most shots have backspin on them; a ball that hits the back rim will pop back, and may land in the basket. A shot that hits the front rim with backspin has no chance to fall in. Finally, a basketball has a nine-inch diameter while the rim has an eighteen-inch diameter; a miss on the long side still has room for a nine-inch margin of error.

Sharman's approach was the same in his pre-game preparation. At USC, from one of his instructors, he learned the notion that when you use and train your muscles, they develop a "memory." He became convinced that by repeating the movements enough, he could develop "memory muscles": he could, in other words, teach his body to "remember" the proper movements for putting a ball in the basket. It was this theory that was to become an important part of Sharman's coaching philosophy—much to the dismay of his less disciplined players. Especially important to Sharman was his discovery that by sharpening his skills on the day of a game, his "memory muscles" would be at their most per-spicacious.

"When we were on the road," Sharman recalls, "me, Frank Ramsey and Gene Conley would like to go over and do some shooting on the day of the game. Red always made sure that we could go over and shoot, that balls were there. I felt looser for the game, with a lot more confidence. I always had a game day routine: eating habits, toilet habits, sleeping habits. The more I did it, the more it helped."

For all his success, however, Bill Sharman never became the local hero that Cousy did. There were special circum-stances, of course. Cousy was a local college player who brought his own constituency to the Celtics, and his style of play was as spectacular as Sharman's was stolid. But Shar-man also became the first Celtic to leave the close-knit group under unhappy circumstances. By 1960, when Sam and K.C. Jones were part of the remarkable Boston backcourt, Shar-man was getting less playing time: 2,382 minutes in the 1958–59 season; 1,916 in 59–60; barely 1,500 in 1960–61. Cousy would later welcome less playing time as a chance to extend his career. Sharman saw it as a threat.

In 1961, at the age of thirty-four, Sharman was concerned about his future. The NBA was going to expand with the addition of Chicago, and Sharman, one of the highest-priced members of the Celtics, was concerned that he would not be protected when the expansion draft took place. Also, he wanted to be a coach. He went to Celtic owner Walter Brown and, as he remembers it, "asked if there was a future for me with the club after my playing days." Brown was making no commitment, because—as Sharman had feared—the Celtics were not planning to protect him in the expansion draft. If his salary dissuaded the new Chicago franchise from taking him, they reasoned, fine. If not, the Celtics still had a strong backcourt between the veteran Cousy—whose popularity alone would have made it suicidal to leave him unprotected —and K.C. and Sam Jones.

Sharman did not stay to find out what Chicago would do. Harlem Globetrotter owner Abe Saperstein, incensed at the NBA for denying him a West Coast franchise he thought had been promised him for years, announced that he was founding a new, rival professional league, the American Basketball League. In part attracted by the chance to return to Southern California, in part determined not to end his playing days as a member of a cellar-dwelling expansion team, Sharman left the Celtics to become coach of the Los Angeles Jets.

His move so angered Walter Brown that the Celtic owner withheld Sharman's $3,400 playoff money from the 1961 title for more than a year, and he sued the ABL when the faltering league tried to put Sharman back into a player's uniform.

Sharman's doggedness and sheer compulsive energy helped make him more successful a coach than any member of the Celtic fraternity except Auerbach himself. But he was also to suffer the kinds of setbacks that no amount of preparation and planning can cope with, the kind of body blows that are never supposed to happen to a Golden Boy.

5

Frank Ramsey and Jim Loscutoff: The Supporting Cast

There are skeptics who claim that Red Auerbach was always an overrated coach, and no one who played with the Boston Celtics ever maintained that he was a technically gifted strategist. The few set plays used by the Celtics were so well-known, for example, that players drawn from teams around the NBA could run them just from having seen them so often.

There is no doubt, however, that throughout his coaching days Auerbach employed a single philosophy of basketball. And one of the key elements of that philosophy was the use of substitutions. In his first years with the Washington Capitals, Auerbach boasted of his team's "failure" to field an NBA scoring leader. Not one of his division-winning Capitals even placed in the top ten. His reserves, Auerbach explained back in 1948, were too good to warm the bench, so no one or two players had to bear the burden of the offense. Further, only a very few players could play forty-five or forty-eight minutes a game. Most players need a good ten to twenty minutes of rest if they are to perform well in a pro game.

As Auerbach said, probably for the ten thousandth time, "I always worked on the theory that when you made your substitutions you shouldn't weaken your team, you should strengthen your team. Your real starting team isn't the team on the floor when the game begins, it's the team on the floor when the game ends. But you gotta be a helluva guy to accept that kind of role."

An ideal sixth man must play with an acute sense of what his team needs. An individualistic player, no matter how gifted, cannot supply the kind of different curatives that a sickly team may require. He must have the patience and the security to give up the "starting" role by which fans often judge the best players on a team.

There are still other attributes for an Auerbach sixth man. He must be in physical and mental condition to come right off the bench, into the flow of a game, and instantly pick up the rhythm and intensity of the game without a warm-up, without the process of feeling out the opposition. He must be able to concentrate on his rival from the bench as intently as if he were playing, watching the rival's moves and weaknesses. And he must have the confidence to move into a game and—as is often the need—take command, ignite the offense, score the big basket, neutralize the hot opponent's hot scorer.

In almost any pro basketball game, even between unequal teams, there will be moments when a big lead is whittled away, or when an offense simply breaks down. That is when the sixth man can change the entire character of a game, speeding up or slowing down the pace, drawing a dominant center away from the basket with accurate outside shooting or creating new scoring opportunities by driving into the middle.

Although Auerbach was not considered an innovator, the concept of a "sixth man" had never been developed until he

came along, and it has been steadily employed by the Boston
Celtics for more than two decades. In short, Auerbach not
only "invented" the position; he refined it and made it a
permanent part of basketball strategy.

Frank Ramsey, who was to become the first sixth man for
Boston, came from Madisonville, Kentucky. He was one of
those athletes no one had ever thought to doubt. Other Celtics always felt some doubt that they belonged on the team,
but no one—including Frank Ramsey—ever seemed to question his worth. In 1948, Ramsey was a high school All-
American at Madisonville High. That year, his team lost in
the state basketball tournament to Owensboro, a team lead
by Cliff Hagan, who was to become a lifelong friend.

His high school heroics led Ramsey to the University of
Kentucky, then the dominant team in college basketball.
Playing under crusty Adolph Rupp, Ramsey became the
quarterback of the Wildcats as a sophomore, leading them
to a 32-2 record and a national championship. The following
year, the team was 29-3, with one of the losses eliminating
them from the NCAA tournament. In 1952–53, Kenctucky
didn't compete at all, having been suspended from all play
for recruiting violations, but the senior players were allowed
an extra year of eligibility.

This suspension afforded Auerbach the opportunity for his
legendary coup at the 1953 draft. Since the Kentucky players
were remaining in school to use their last year of eligibility,
none of the NBA teams even thought of the Wildcat squad
as part of the draft. But Auerbach picked three starters—
Ramsey, Cliff Hagan and Lou Tsioropoulous—on successive
rounds. The draft rule stated only that a player was eligible
for the draft if his entering class had graduated. So the league
let Auerbach have his coup but clarified that rule for future
years.

In that season at Kentucky, Ramsey led his team to an

unbeaten season and conference championship. And when he showed up at Boston, he gave no sign of doubting his ability. "He was cocky as hell," Bob Brannum says, "but you had to like him. Rookies on the Celtics are usually quiet, shy, but Ramsey just kept telling everyone, 'Hey, I'm good, you *know* I'm gonna make this team.' And he was right."

When Ramsey scored 24 points against New York, a reporter asked Knick coach Joe Lapchick if it wasn't an impressive performance for a rookie. Ramsey, the coach snapped, was never a rookie. In fact, a sense of self-confidence seems to have been Frank Ramsey's trademark. Not boasting, not self-congratulations, but rather a natural acknowledgment of the fact that he was a very good player.

Probably his best-known single play occurred in the deciding game of the 1957 playoffs. In the second overtime, with the Celtics holding a 1-point lead, Ramsey threw up an off-balance, twenty-foot one-hander that assured Boston's first title. Yet Ramsey played a more significant role in the opening round of the same playoffs against Syracuse. In the last two games, he guarded Nat scoring ace Dolph Schayes and held him to two field goals. Schayes was six-foot-eight; Ramsey, six-three.

This ability to make up for height was an important asset for the sixth man as employed by Auerbach. In the early championship years, Ramsey was a third guard, and he could use his height to shoot over an opponent without giving up too much speed. But when Sam Jones arrived, making the Celtics guard-rich, Ramsey showed his versatility by playing in the corners. He used his head—the inside of it—to get position on his man and take more rebounds than his size would suggest. Playing against a bigger forward, he used his speed to quickly cut down the rival's height and muscle advantage.

Ramsey rarely started a game. He would be on the bench as the starting forward combination of Loscutoff and Hein-

sohn pounded away for five or ten minutes. Then he would
go in and usually play for a shade under thirty minutes,
averaging in his peak seasons (1958–62) 15 or 16 points a
game. His very presence was a potent psychological weapon.
Tom Heinsohn, the high-scoring, low-stamina forward, did
not have to worry about pacing himself, about trying to rest
on the court, particularly on defense—a cardinal Celtic sin.
Instead, he could shoot, rebound and muscle the opposition
with abandon, knowing that when he was out of breath a
first-rate player would be coming off the bench for him. The
opposition knew all too well that when Heinsohn went out,
the Celtics were giving up very little power. Ex-teammates
remember him, in the words of one, as "the damnedest
clutch player you ever saw."

Apart from his on-the-court play, Ramsey seemed to give
the Celtics a sense of stability. From his earliest days, he had
been fascinated by money and investment matters, and veteran Celtics frequently consulted him about arcane questions
concerning Wall Street. Before a crucial playoff game, he
would remind his teammates that they were playing with his
money. He was not joking: he carefully computed the playoff
pool, so that he knew exactly how much he (and the others)
had to gain by winning.

And if Frank Ramsey was looking for a psychological
prod for his teammates, he was also searching for an edge
against his rivals. His one brush with controversy came in
1963, when he wrote a piece for *Sports Illustrated* explaining
the "finer points of basketball strategy." Those points included specific techniques for drawing fouls that hadn't
really been committed, and for turning charges into blocks
and blocks into charges.

"Drawing fouls," Ramsey wrote, "requires the ability to
provide good, heartwarming drama, and to direct it to the
right audience [the referee]." He told how he shifted his
weight so that his body moved in front of an offensive player

while his feet were to one side—thus turning a blocking violation against himself into a charging foul against his opponent. He advised hook shooters to drop their non-shooting arms to their sides, letting their opponents come down on top of them.

The article got Ramsey a verbal lashing from NBA Commissioner Walter Kennedy, who called it "a very irresponsible act by a mature professional athlete." It was perhaps the only visible mistake Ramsey committed in his nine years with Boston.

At the end of the 1964 season, Ramsey announced his retirement from professional basketball—for reasons that are typically atypical. In contrast to athletes who can't find the extra step, or who get beaten on defense, Ramsey simply had too much waiting for him in Madisonville. A home-building project had turned into a thriving construction business, and Ramsey said that he'd gotten on several planes that year to make a trip and started to think about his construction business instead of who the Celtics were playing that night. "A pro shouldn't think that way," he concluded.

•

Auerbach employed, or claimed he employed, a welter of "psych" tactics, designed to anger the opposition and fire up his team. The lighting of the victory cigar was a way of expressing superiority over the other team, and another element for opponents to worry about when the game wound down: "God, I don't want to see that cigar." So was getting himself thrown out of a game in which the Celtics were hopelessly behind; it was Auerbach's belief that the players always wanted to prove they could win without him, and would thus be inspired to fight back from a 20-point deficit.

Similarly, Auerbach used psychological warfare with his players after considering them case by case. When he judged that a player needed coddling, he would never criticize the man, always praising him for good plays and ignoring the bad. But when he believed a player needed a fire lit under him to be motivated, he could be mercilessly unfair in his attack. Among his victims, none took a harder riding—and none expresses more affection for Auerbach—than Jim Loscutoff.

Loscutoff came to the Celtics in 1955 from the University of Oregon, where he had led the Northern Division of the Pacific Coast Conference with a 19.6 scoring average and was on the All-Conference first team. The first round draft choice of the Celtics was less than overwhelmed with his selection by Boston; NBA basketball being what it was twenty years ago, the draft did not cause college seniors, high school phenoms, or agents (of both player and Internal Revenue variety) to wait anxiously by their telephones.

"When I was in college," Loscutoff recalls, "they called and told me they had drafted me number one, and asked if I would be interested in playing pro ball. I said, 'Draft what? What the hell's a draft?' There was no Celtic legend. There was no Auerbach legend. The only legend was Bob Cousy, who was Mr. Basketball. They had just started televising pro ball in '54, and I remember after a college game in Idaho we went over to a fraternity house, and we watched Cousy score fifty points in that four-overtime game against Syracuse. That got me a little interested.

"I was going to play AAU ball, which was the big thing then, because you had job security with a company. The Gulf Oilers were interested in me, so I decided to ask for a ridiculous amount of money. Like eight thousand dollars. So they said okay, with a $500 bonus, which I took and went and put a down payment on a car. I wish now I'd asked for more."

There may well have been times when Loscutoff was tempted to aim that car straight for the lobby of the Hotel Lenox at about the time his coach would be leaving for

Boston Garden. Without a doubt, Auerbach made Loscutoff's life more miserable than that of any Celtic opponent. John Mahnken, one of the old Caps who played for Auerbach in Washington, the Tri-Cities and Boston, was the first of his scapegoats, and Tommy Heinsohn may later have passed Loscutoff's record for number of undeserved attacks, but Loscutoff was the first long-term Auerbach whipping boy. Opponents who recoiled at his intensity and his physical aggressiveness, and writers who nicknamed him "Jungle Jim Loscutoff," probably never imagined that he saw the face of his coach on each of his victims—or that he vowed repeatedly, "When I quit this team, the first thing I'm going to do is to drag Auerbach into an alley and beat the hell out of him."

From a perspective of more than ten years away from the Celtic locker room, Loscutoff speaks with a very different tone: "He was going through us to relate to the other guys. It was very difficult for him to chew out Bob Cousy or Bill Russell or Bill Sharman or Frank Ramsey. So what he'd do is go through Tommy Heinsohn or myself to relate to the other guys.

"We could play a hell of a half, and come in at half time and get our ass chewed. He would tell us what we were doing wrong, and yet *we* were doing it right. Russell or Cousy might be doing it wrong, but he'd never say, 'Cousy, you're doing that wrong,' or 'Russell, you're doing this wrong.' They were smart enough to pick up from what Red was saying to us what he was trying to tell them."

Loscutoff averaged 10.6 points a game during the Celtics' first championship season. But in the fall of 1957, he suffered a severe knee injury, and played only five games the entire season. At training in 1958, Auerbach put his bully-boy technique to work—and Loscutoff believes it saved his career.

"When I made a comeback," he says, "I was apprehensive. I was scared that if I jumped, my whole knee was going to be thrown out. Christ, he had me like an animal. He was throwing the ball on the floor, and I was chasing it, diving for the ball on the floor. He made it a comical thing. He used to call the other players over and say, 'Watch this,' and he'd throw the ball on the floor and I'd dive after it. It was a confidence-builder; it really helped me psychologically, and I don't think I'd have made it if it wasn't for that."

Loscutoff played six more seasons—every one of them on championship teams. And while he never averaged much in the way of scoring (his career game average with Boston was 6.2 points), his presence, and his reputation as a "floor cop" who would even up any rough stuff committed against the Cousys and the Sharmans, kept a lot of games honest. "I like my reputation," he says. "I like it when somebody gets belted in an Olympic game and Keith Jackson says to a world-wide audience, 'Shades of Jim Loscutoff!' But it was always a little exaggerated."

For Loscutoff, as with just about every other alumnus of the Celtics, the Auerbach method was not a highly technical basketball clinic. "There were no detailed drills, as far as that was concerned," he remembers. "The only thing we had extensive practices on was the fast-break situation."

And the break, like diamonds, is forever. "It's the same fast break they have right now," Loscutoff says. "We always looked for Cousy, and our release pass was around the key of the defensive boards. If we got a rebound on this end of the court, Cooz would always be right around the key, so we'd look for him. Now what they're doing is releasing the ball a little further out, almost toward the half-court line. But the pattern is the same. You take the ball to the middle, because you can look from the right to the left. Cowens is terrific at getting the ball in midair and releasing it while turning, if the rebound is uncontested. And Russell was even better."

As for technical details, says Loscutoff, Auerbach was

limited. "If you sat down with Red and said to him, 'How about designing a zone defense that will offset this person over here,' he couldn't do that. He could not write x's and o's. A lot of the innovations the Celtics had were things we did in college. The players would say to Red, 'Let's try this, let's try that.' Red had five basic plays. We'd run through them a half-hour, forty-five minutes a day. He always used to say, 'Never blame a play. If it goes wrong, it's the player's fault.'

"But Red really knew psychology. Like, he knew that if one or two guys got quick baskets, the adrenaline starts to go, and you're starting to motivate yourself. He used to do it a lot in the third quarter, always used to say, 'Let's go out and win the third quarter,' or 'Just win the second half.' And he knew exactly what he needed; that's why he let Hagan and Macauley go in '56 to get an unestablished player like Bill Russell. Because he knew he could never win without the big man. And it worked; once we were champions, we got to the point where we believed we were the best team that was ever established on a basketball court. We felt we could turn a game anytime we wanted to. That's why Auerbach always used to draft winners. He thought, 'If you're a loser, you're going to be a loser.'

I asked Loscutoff to speculate on how Auerbach might have done in another field besides basketball. "That's hard to say." He grinned. "He's obnoxious with people, so in a situation where he wasn't so much in the limelight, he'd have to change his whole personality. Everybody's been kissing his ass for years and years and years. You know, no matter what, he always treats you bad when he first sees you. I was over at the Garden for a playoff game, and he had some sandwiches in his office, and when I walked in, he started growling, 'Dammit, those aren't for you, they're for my guests.' But that's a lot of show. He's a sentimental old slob, and the older he gets, the more sentimental he gets. He loves to reminisce, especially with an audience."

Loscutoff seems to have one regret about his career, and about that of his teammates: their playing days happened too soon. "I played nine years," he says. "My top salary was fifteen thousand dollars, and my top playoff money was four thousand. You sit back and listen to these guys who are on the bench drawing ninety thousand, a hundred thousand, with the retirement benefits. I have a lot of animosity now. The athlete today is like a movie star. So much in demand, so many people who idolize him. Heroes, especially white heroes, are very few and far between . . . I think I was fifteen years too soon."

He also wonders what might have happened if the Celtics had been appreciated by their town: "We used to go out there and see the empty seats, and it burned the shit out of us. We used to say that if we had that dynasty in a city like New York, we'd all be rich. Even a guy like Mr. Cousy never really capitalized on his ability. People sometimes say too much has been made about the Celtic dynasty. I don't think enough has. There's never been anything like it in pro sports. And they're finally getting recognition. But you can see what it's meant to us. If you're an ex-Celtic, and you locate here, you've been so successful at basketball, you don't want to demean yourself by failing."

•

Loscutoff and Ramsey, Cousy and Sharman. These were the four pre-championship Celtics. The other regulars on those teams were gone before the fall of 1956. Bob Brannum, who has remained close to the Celtics and coaches at Brandeis University outside Boston, retired after the 1955 playoffs. He was a rugged combative player, a forerunner of Loscutoff.

Ed Macauley and Cliff Hagan, of course, wound up in St. Louis—they were the price Auerbach had to pay for the rights to Bill Russell. Macauley was near the end of his playing days, but he remained with the Hawks long enough to share the 1958 championship with them. Hagan had been drafted from Kentucky with Ramsey, but had been in the service and never played a game in the Celtic uniform. He played ten years for the Hawks and then jumped to the ABA.

As the 1956–57 season opened, it was not yet clear that a dynasty had been born. For years, fans in Boston had been hoping for a championship. Now they saw four of their old stand-bys returning. Their highly publicized new center, Bill Russell, was away playing in the Olympics and wouldn't join the team until late November. The only other addition was a rookie named Tommy Heinsohn.

6

Tommy Heinsohn: The Stepchild

By the conventional measurements of success, Tommy Heinsohn ranks with the most notable members of the remarkable fraternity of Boston Celtics. From his earliest playing days in city gymnasiums and youth centers, he was celebrated as a first-rate basketball player. As a high school star, he was besieged by scholarship offers and college recruiters. As a collegian, he was an All-American. As a pro, he was six times picked for an All-Star team, and in his nine-year career with the Celtics he played on eight NBA championship teams, three times leading his club in scoring. He was a clutch player of astonishing dimensions; frequently, he was the difference between a playoff victory and defeat. He retired to become a successful insurance executive, then came back to his old team when the dynasty collapsed, to serve as their coach.

These cold facts, however, conceal as much as they reveal. For Tom Heinsohn consistently served another function as a Celtic: he was a scapegoat, a figure who never earned the full measure of respect to which he was entitled. By a series of circumstances, Heinsohn was the Celtics' lightning rod, the stepchild, the man who took the abuse of his coach, the other players, the fans, and—at one point—the team's owner as well. And if his personality and behavior at times seemed to draw this treatment, it is more true that Heinsohn served as a scapegoat out of necessity. Whether in an office, a college dormitory, a combat platoon, or any other small group, some figure must serve as a target for the frustrations and hostilities of others; someone must absorb the free-lance anger that is part of any group of people thrown together in a common pursuit. Because of the nature of the people who ran and played with the Celtics—and because of his on-the-court job and his off-the-court behavior, so different from that of the other Celtics—Tom Heinsohn inherited that role, and never shed it. It is perhaps a measure of his true character that he has lived with that thankless task for twenty years.

It is often said that "even paranoids have real enemies." And if Heinsohn sometimes hears the sound of hostility where there is none—in a referee's call, in a writer's column —perhaps it is because he has never, and may never, have a chance to be judged on his own, without the pervasive presence of living ghosts.

Tom Heinsohn was born in 1934 in Union City, New Jersey. His father was a supervisor in a baking plant; his mother, an inventory clerk in a dime store. It was not an affluent childhood. "If it weren't for basketball," he once said, "I'd probably be working on the docks."

Heinsohn knew the feeling of outside hostility early in life. As the only child of a German family in an Irish and Italian neighborhood, he was the logical target of hostility from other children when World War II broke out. He recalled once, half-jokingly, "I didn't go out of the house from the time I was five until I was twelve years old."

His first real taste of competitive basketball came during his participation in games at an after-school community center under the guidance of one-time Villanova great, Perry Del Purgatorio. That particular CYO gym in Jersey City had an important influence on Heinsohn's career: because of its low roof, Heinsohn developed a jump shot with an unusually straight trajectory. The no-arc jump shot was to become one of his principal offensive weapons.

As a playground star, Heinsohn got a scholarship to St. Michael's High School, where Pat Finnegan of Fordham University fame was his coach. By the time his high school days were over, he had been named a schoolboy All-American and had received more than 200 scholarship offers. His choice was clearly pragmatic. "I picked Holy Cross as my college so that I could be the territorial draft pick of the Celtics," he said years later.

He quickly established himself as a driving, competitive figure, as a basketball player and student. He made the dean's list; his paintings won school prizes; as a freshman, he captained an undefeated squad in the 1952–53 season. "The thing about Tommy," classmate Joe Reilly remembers, "is that he was one fellow you were sure would never be satisfied unless he finished on top in everything he attended."

His reputation grew throughout his college career: as a sophomore, he was the second highest Crusader scorer, finishing behind Togo Palazzi; as a junior, he played as both a pivot and outside man, which sharpened his shooting eye, and he was named Most Valuable Player at the Sugar Bowl tournament. And as a senior, he led his team to a 22-5 record and won for himself an All-American berth.

And yet, as soon as Heinsohn entered the orbit of the Celtics, the team he had sought to join as a high school star, the distance between himself and full acceptance into the Boston fraternity began to be established. His selection as a first-round draft choice was overshadowed by the news that

Auerbach had given up Ed Macauley and Cliff Hagan for the rights to Bill Russell, the nation's most prominent collegian. It was the big man, the rebounder, the shot-blocker, who was going to lead the Celtics to a title, along with the high-priced superstars Bob Cousy and Bill Sharman. Heinsohn's selection was clearly the story on page two.

And Auerbach was already publicly admonishing Heinsohn for excess weight and his occasional habit of relaxing on the court. "Heinsohn will never make it with the Celtics if he continues to pace himself as he did with the Cross," he told the press before he had signed the six-seven forward to a contract. "He'll have to push himself every minute."

Although Heinsohn claims to have aimed for the Celtics from the beginning, he became sufficiently dubious about his future with the team to consider an offer to play for the Peoria Caterpillars in the AAU's industrial league. (The league, sponsored by companies who gave players jobs in management while they played basketball, was considered an alternative to the still low-salaried NBA.) But, acting on the advice of a fellow Holy Cross alumnus, Bob Cousy, Heinsohn returned to Boston and signed with the Celtics.

In his very first year, however, Heinsohn showed that he belonged. He averaged more than 16 points a game—twelfth in the league in scoring—and was named NBA Rookie of the Year. Moreover, Heinsohn played as important a role as any Celtic in the seven-game victory over the St. Louis Hawks which gave Boston its first championship. In the fifth game, Heinsohn scored 23 points to give the Celtics a 124–109 victory. And in the deciding two-overtime 125–123 victory, in which both Cousy and Sharman went cold, Heinsohn scored 37 points and pulled down 23 rebounds. A rookie, he was the coolest player on the court.

Throughout his nine seasons, Heinsohn delivered the clutch play in critical situations with impressive consistency. In the sixth and final game against Philadelphia in the 1960

Eastern finals, he won the game by tipping in a Sharman miss. In the 1963 final round, in the fourth game against Los Angeles, he scored 35 points—including three baskets within a minute—and iced the title in the sixth game by sinking four straight pressure free throws in the closing seconds. In that same contest, he stole a pass from Jerry West and scored an uncontested lay-up for 2 critical points. Those heroics came on top of a first-game performance in which he scored the last 6 points of a 3-point victory, and a 26-point performance in the second game.

A year later, facing the San Francisco Warriors and Wilt Chamberlain, Heinsohn turned the fourth game around: with the Celtics trailing by a point, he hit a 3-point play, then a tip-in, then a jump shot. Then, following two K.C. Jones free throws, he hit a jump shot, a hook, a running hook, and a lay-up off a fast break. Boston had an 11-point lead, the game, and a 3–1 lead.

The skills that produced these results—and his career-long 18.6 scoring average, his 12,194 points, his 5,749 rebounds—were essentially offensive. His low-trajectory shot was unusual, and opponents had great difficulty adjusting to it. In addition, he had a devastating hook shot, accurate from twenty feet or more in contrast to the five to fifteen-foot range of most other hook shooters. Bill Sharman, one of the most consistent and scientific shooters in basketball history, once said, "Tommy has the greatest variety of effective shots in the league. There are better shooters, I suppose, but Tommy's agility and his exceptional body control give him a big advantage."

Heinsohn himself saw his skills as a natural complement to those of his teammates. "Since Cooz would rather pass than shoot, and since I'd rather shoot than pass, we got along beautifully," he observed shortly before his retirement in 1965. "Sharman preferred to work out of the right corner, and I worked out of the left. After Cousy retired, I had to change my style of play, because we no longer had the guards to run the team the way he did. Our power was in the backcourt with Sam Jones and John Havlicek. So I don't try to score as much, but pass more, defend better, and try to set up the other fellows with pick-offs and blocks." Moreover, Heinsohn was particularly skilled at moving inside the battle under the offensive boards to tip in missed shots.

Given this kind of performance, Heinsohn should have had a reputation among Celtics fans much like Tommy Heinrich did with Yankee followers: that of an "Old Reliable" who came through in the clutch, who anchored his team with consistently effective offense. He deserves recognition as a key figure that turned potential defeats into victories, that gave Boston its incredible string of eight consecutive world championships.

But that is not what Tom Heinsohn stands for in the story of the Celtics. He is instead a figure who is not taken totally seriously; who is treated with a hint of amusement and condescension in the chronicles of the Celtics. The reasons for this provide a revealing clue, in an ironic way, to the success of the Celtics over the years. Deliberately or not, Heinsohn was cast as a kind of outsider, a player whose style and attitude were in contrast to those of his teammates and coach.

One of the principal explanations for the Celtic record is that Auerbach's teams were made up of players who were in better condition than their rivals. Players who came to Boston after years with other clubs, like Carl Braun and Willie Naulls, expressed disbelief in the pace of the training camps. Auerbach himself points out that while other teams were playing themselves into shape after the season began, Boston was building insurmountable leads by Christmas time. The players themselves were committed to the system, either by individual training or by fear of Auerbach's wrath. Bill Sharman used to begin long-distance running weeks before training camp began; John Havlicek lived by a strict regimen of diet and exercise.

Heinsohn, by contrast, came to the Celtics twenty pounds overweight (by Auerbach's judgment, not his college coach's) and sluggish. And Auerbach never stopped harassing him for being short-winded and too heavy. "I got on his back and never got off," Auerbach boasted once. "I felt I had to do it to get the maximum out of him." The players quickly picked up on this theme; Bill Russell once publicly advised the coach to pour a bucket of ice water over Heinsohn until he picked himself up and started running. The image of Heinsohn as an out-of-shape player continued until his retirement in 1965—when Auerbach characterized him as having "the oldest twenty-nine-year-old body in the world."

Second, Heinsohn was a shooter. In his career in Boston, he shot the ball 19,303 times—roughly two shots every three playing minutes. His fondness for the shot was legendary among his teammates, who nicknamed him "Tommygun" and "Ack-Ack," and who teased him with lines like Bob Cousy's famous crack: "I'll say this for Tommy—he never shot unless he had the ball."

This reputation is highly misleading. Heinsohn was not walking onto the court and flinging the ball up with abandon. He played on a team whose center, Bill Russell, was not a shooter, and with players such as K.C. Jones and Tom Sanders, whose primary responsibilities were defensive. More than once, Heinsohn asked Auerbach whether he was shooting too frequently, and Auerbach told him, in effect, to keep shooting until he was told not to. But the presence of so persistent a shooter on a team that made defense its watchword once again placed Heinsohn outside of the mainstream of Celtic personalities. And the unorthodox style of his shots, particular his running, long-distance hook, made it seem as if Heinsohn was sometimes shooting indiscriminately.

One particular incident cost Heinsohn a measure of popularity in Boston. In 1964, the NBA All-Star game was coming to Boston for the first time since the Celtic dynasty had blossomed. For Walter Brown, the owner of the Celtics, it was a proud moment. He had created the All-Star game in 1951, and bankrolled it himself to prove its box-office potential to a skeptical league. And the Celtics, into which he had put all of his energy and money, had become the premiere team in sports history. To bring the All-Star game over national television from the arena that his father had run before him, that represented his life's work, was a moment of total satisfaction for Brown. Almost.

For months before the January exhibition, the NBA Players' Association had been seeking an agreement from the owners for a pension plan. The president of the association was Tom Heinsohn, who had taken the reins over when the founder of the group, Bob Cousy, got fed up in the struggle for recognition and players' benefits. After months of indifference by the owners, the Association finally decided on a drastic course of action: without some kind of agreement, there would be no All-Star game. It fell to Heinsohn to inform Walter Brown of this decision.

Following a twenty-minute delay, and a personal locker-room promise by NBA Commissioner Walter Kennedy that a pension agreement would be forthcoming, the All-Stars took the court. But to Walter Brown, who regarded the Celtics as a family, and who had prided himself on treating his players and employees fairly, without the compulsion of formal agreements, the act of the players was a deep personal wound. The next morning, he publicly attacked Heinsohn as "the number one heel in all my association with sports" and vowed never again to go into a Celtic locker room. That vow lasted all of three weeks, and Brown and Heinsohn made up after Boston won the NBA title. But Walter Brown had two generations of tradition behind him in Boston, and was by all accounts one of the best-loved figures—in or out of sports

—in the entire community. No one who took on Brown, even out of principle, could come out on top, and the dispute drove a hidden wedge between Heinsohn and much of the Boston press corps.

Finally, Tom Heinsohn's personality and attitude *seemed* to be at sharp variance with those of the other Celtics. In the dynasty years, the skeptical, outspoken athlete was still an anomaly. Most of the Celtics were very much in the tradition of what we expect our gladiators to be: fiercely dedicated, totally competitive, possessed of the will to win, taciturn and driven.

Heinsohn was competitive, all right, to the point of challenging some of the NBA's toughest figures when play got rough (he once almost slugged it out with Wilt Chamberlain, and Wilt once broke his hand during a playoff game attempting to punch Heinsohn). In fact, he played with an openly aggressive attitude, mouth curled, hands on hips, arguing with opponents and referees.

But Heinsohn was different from the conventional image of the athlete. He was a reader, a painter, a would-be writer, something of an intellectual in the world of the jock. He was also a raconteur, a humorist, a contentious talker who has probably kept the lights on in more hotel coffee shops in more NBA cities than any ten salesmen. He was assertive, voluble, the kind of personality who would be at home in a law school lounge, arguing about everything from foreign policy to the fine print in a contracts case. And he was also able to put some distance between himself and the do-or-die image of athletes in general, and the Celtics in particular. In his book *The Last Loud Roar*, Bob Cousy contrasts his own killer rage building before a climactic playoff game with Heinsohn's casual wanderings around town, and his invitation to tour an electronics plant. And among athletes with some very clear views about masculinity, Heinsohn once showed up at a costume party in a Little Lord Fauntleroy outfit, complete with lollipop. It was unconventional behavior—outrageous in a sense, but not the kind that reinforces the "good old boy" sensibility most athletes adopt.

All of this was reflected in Auerbach's treatment of Heinsohn. Knowing that Russell would not stand for criticism, that Cousy had once called his bluff and suggested a trade back in 1953, that Sharman would be offended by it, Auerbach had to find a player through whom he could pass his criticisms; for nine years, Tommy Heinsohn was that player. He was yelled at in practices, in the locker room, at time-outs, at half time; he was charged not just with his own sins, but with the failures of the Celtic "untouchables." Heinsohn understood what was going on, and Auerbach would always praise him for his play, his intelligence, his courage. Nonetheless, as any scapegoat from a classroom or summer camp can testify, the persistent assaults of the authority figure have a way of trickling down, and neither teammates nor the press could give Heinsohn his full measure of respect. As a consequence, he was frequently passed over in the accounts of Celtic games, just as he was passed up for the All-Star team because of the league's "three-men-to-a-team" rule; Heinsohn placed fourth to Russell, Cousy and Sharman, even if he was one of the NBA's best forwards.

Heinsohn would frequently shrug off his lack of recognition. "A couple of times a year, it really gets me down," he once said. "Things like scoring thirty or thirty-five points a game and then getting one line of ink at the tail end of the story . . . But why worry about it? My time will come."

It has been almost twenty years now since Tommy Heinsohn arrived at the Boston Celtics' training camp; a decade or more since he hung up his shoes for the last time. He has, with the single exception of Auerbach himself, remained as a part of the Celtic team, taking on and succeeding with thankless tasks.

And he is still waiting for his time to come.

7

Bill Russell: The Giant-Killer

Big-time sports is a ruthless winnower of talent. Young men who dazzled their high school and college audiences arrive at training camps every year expecting immortality over-night. Many are cut within a few days and leave with nothing but a ticket home. Players who find a low rung on the profes-sional ladder spend years as benchwarmers, trade-bait, jour-neymen who do not know from one month to the next what city they will be living in. For a far smaller number, sports is the path to honors, trophies, awards, good money, and an immortality of sorts in the Hall of Fame, the Old-Timers' games, the Great Moments books.

And then there is the ultimate level, reserved for those players who not only perform brilliantly, but whose presence so dominates a game that it is irrevocably altered. These players change strategies, and redefine the way we look at a game, the way an artist changes our expectations about what we see or read or hear. In baseball, for example, Babe Ruth taught fans to rejoice in the presence of sheer power, power that obliterated strategy by the simple expedient of hitting the ball beyond the reach of everyone; others participated in more championships—at least if they were members of the New York Yankees—or had more talent, or may have even contributed to the process of victory more than Ruth did, but he changed the frame of reference forever.

Less than half a dozen basketball players can be placed in this category. Hank Luisetti, the Stanford great, popularized the jump shot, which—when brought to the pros by Jumping Joe Fulks of the Philadelphia Warriors, the first NBA champions—made offenses quicker and more flexible. This, in turn, forced a radical change in defensive theory, since players had to keep closer to their rivals. George Mikan established, first at DePaul and later with the Minneapolis Lakers, that a big man with athletic ability could quickly build a powerful offensive team; later, Wilt Chamberlain was to prove the same point. Bob Cousy, in his turn, showed that proximity to the floor could be an asset rather than a social disease.

If there is a first among equals in this category, that designation must go to Bill Russell, the center of the Celtics for every one of their thirteen dynasty years. Twice in those years Boston did *not* win the NBA championship, and in one of those years Russell was injured through the final three games of the championship series. Only once, against the 1967 Philadelphia 76ers, was Boston beaten by an unquestionably better team. Moreover, the championship quality that Russell exemplified was not confined to the Celtics: from his junior year in college through his last year with the Celtics, Bill Russell played on thirteen of fifteen possible championship teams, not including the Olympic team he led to a Gold Medal in 1956.

This record, however, does not measure the full stature of Bill Russell, nor wholly explain his landslide victory in the voting for Player of the Decade, 1961–70 (he beat runner-up

THE TEAM. The 1964–65 Celtics gather around bald-headed Red Auerbach during a time-out. In the immediate circle from his left are John Havlicek, Sam Jones (24), Tom Sanders (16), K.C. Jones (25), Bill Russell (6) and Tom Heinsohn (15).

CONTINUITY. *Above,* the team celebrates its first championship in 1957. *At right,* the early Celtic brain trust consults on the bench. *Top right,* the team celebrates a seventh title in 1964, and *at far right* coach Tom Heinsohn and veteran John Havlicek toast their 1974 victory, the team's twelfth.

THE GUARDS. The Celtics had four of the great backcourt men in the game's history. *Across top,* defensive specialist K.C. Jones, scorer Bill Sharman, playmaker Bob Cousy and scorer-playmaker Sam Jones.

THE SWING MEN. The dynasty teams always had a sixth man who could play either guard or forward. *Below,* Frank Ramsey; *at right,* John Havlicek.

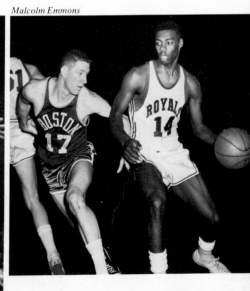

THE CENTER. The one man who played for every dynasty team was Bill Russell, a man of many moods and talents. *Counterclockwise from left,* he displays his defensive genius, his sense of humor, his weariness as player-coach, and his watchfulness against giant Wilt Chamberlain.

THE FORWARDS. Tom Heinsohn, *right,* spent nine seasons with dynasty teams and was called back to coach in 1970. *Below,* Jim Loscutoff, Don Nelson and Tom Sanders.

Malcolm Emmons

Malcolm Emmons

Malcolm Emmons

Malcolm Em

THE PRESENT. In 1976, an old face—John Havlicek—and a new one—Dave Cowens—help bring another championship to Boston. *Below*, three generations of Celtic leaders—Red Auerbach, Tom Heinsohn and Havlicek—accept the familiar trophy.

UPI

Wilt Chamberlain by a 3–1 landslide). Russell, after all, played with a superb aggregation of players. It was always Chamberlain's claim that Boston repeatedly beat his teams because they had better players and, usually, better coaching. And however one measures the individual basketball skills of the two men, the Celtics as a team were clearly superior to most of the teams Chamberlain played with.

It was Bill Russell's influence over the game of basketball that makes him unique. For Russell changed the expectations of players, coaches and fans by introducing an essentially new element to the game. One of basketball's delights is that the juxtaposition of big, fast athletes in a terribly constricted physical space breaks the game down into quick elements, usually lasting a few seconds. The ball is brought downcourt, the defense sets up, the ball begins to weave its way toward the shooter, the defense seeks to hamper the process, the shot is taken.

Put simply, Russell changed this chain of events. He showed that an act of will, joined to an act of skill, could turn a good shot into a bad shot, nullify the entire offensive labor —indeed, convert it into a quick basket for the opposing team. His defensive presence altered the basic flow of the game. All of the traditional scoring methods—the lob pass into the big center, the penetration of a guard posting a smaller opponent, the back-door play—were subject to instant nullification by the presence of Russell, who forced the offense in professional basketball to adjust to this defensive threat. And those adjustments, in turn resulting in a faster game and the development of big men with outside shooting skills, altered the flow of the game to this day.

Metaphysicians among us might regard Bill Russell as the living embodiment of Red Auerbach's dream, a theory come to life. Auerbach had spent a decade of frustration, developing a theory of winning basketball he could not demonstrate to its only acceptable conclusion: a championship. It was as if Auerbach had invented the internal combustion engine, only to be told that he was not to be allowed the use of gasoline to demonstrate his invention. When Russell came to Boston, he was trained to play basketball as it might have happened if Auerbach had controlled his destiny.

And if the match-up of theoretician and practitioner was not enough, the final piece of the Hollywood story line is that the man who pointed out Bill Russell to Red Auerbach was Bill Reinhart, the one man Auerbach acknowledges as his mentor, his hero, his intellectual forebear. The same man who had taught Red Auerbach the theory of winning basketball tipped off Auerbach—early, before the national acclaim —about the man who could put that theory into practice.

Finally, Russell's career has consistently carried with it a fascination beyond his remarkable athletic achievements. His public life revolved around two issues that caused him to probe some of our deepest national ills. The first was the strained relationship between a public figure and the public, a consequence of our mass communications and our hunger for public heroes. The second—and by far the more consequential—was the question of race. Russell was the first black superstar in professional basketball in a time when segregation was a matter of law throughout a quarter of the nation and a matter of custom in much of the rest. And he was simply unwilling to conceal his rage. His combination of fame and aloofness, race and rage, made him our first vilified hero. Today, the presence of black pride or outspokenness in an athlete is commonplace. But Russell was the first black star to step outside the role our athletes had always occupied. He demanded to be taken on his own terms, and in the mid-1950's the consumers of sport could not accept that demand. And thus the man who played the most critical role in making the Boston Celtics into sports' greatest dynasty was also partly responsible for denying the team its audience.

William Fenton Russell was born in Monroe, Louisiana, in 1934. When he was nine years old, his parents moved to Oakland, California. Russell's family was poor. When he moved to Boston to join the Celtics, he built an elaborate electric train set in his basement. He remembered a time in his early childhood when he coveted a $15 train set in a store. "That was more than my father was making in a week," he said.

Russell's father, a man he always wrote and spoke of with pride, had begun to move up in California, operating a trucking concern to serve farmers in the San Joacquin Valley. But then Russell's mother died at the age of thirty-two, and his father took a lower-paying factory job to stay closer to his children. Russell was still a child when he came across a book that told the story of Henri Christophe, the liberator of Haiti. "He was mad, he was a despot," Russell recalls in his autobiography, *Go Up for Glory.* "Yet in my young mind, this was the first identification with a Negro who was a leader . . . he was the first hero of my youth, a black man who became the dominant force in a power structure."

Russell did not come from the class of dazzling, liquidly graceful black playground athletes. He did not play basketball until he was at McClymonds High School, and he was at first too awkward and ill-coordinated to make the varsity.

"These guys are just better than me," he told the janitor. "I couldn't make it."

The janitor replied, in a conversation which either did take place or should have, "If you think so, Russell, they always will be."

McClymonds High was an all-black school whose administrators were very aware of potential racial trouble when their teams played white teams. The coach would tell his young players that if trouble ever broke out, it would be labeled a riot and they would be held responsible. The teams he coached took the lesson to heart, winning the local sports-manship award three years running.

Russell's play was not good enough to win him a scholar-ship to a major basketball school. But he did receive one from the University of San Francisco, whose basketball stature could be gauged by the fact that it did not have a home gymnasium ("the Homeless Dons," the press nicknamed them). Russell roomed there with a young man one year ahead of him named K.C. Jones, who was too shy to speak to Russell for a month, but who used some of his scholarship money to keep Russell in food and shoes.

The University of San Francisco was coached by Phil Woolpert, who worshiped at the shrine of Defense. "To me," he once said, "run-and-shoot basketball is only half a game. It's like the Yankees taking batting practice and calling it a baseball game." Woolpert, who had no recruiting attractions at all (twelve of his sixteen players were from the Bay Area), compensated by drilling his team on the basics of defense: steals, overplaying men to deny them the ball, breaking the offensive rhythm, forcing them out of patterns. And once he saw the potential of Russell on defense, he seized the oppor-tunity, instructing his guards to gamble, to overplay with abandon, to go for the steal even at the risk of losing their man, or encouraging a back-door play—because with Rus-sell guarding the middle, there was an insurance policy wait-ing by the basket. That same philosophy would soon be working for the Celtics.

After losing to UCLA early in the 1954–55 season, the University of San Francisco embarked on a fifty-six-game winning streak—then an all-time record. The streak included two straight NCAA titles (over LaSalle and Iowa), and by the time Russell had left USF, the NCAA basketball rules committee was busily at work. Russell had developed a "steer shot," grabbing the errant shots of teammates on the downward arc and steering them into the basket. This led to the offensive goal-tending rule, which forbids any touching of the ball on the downward arc, and the lanes were widened to twelve feet to limit the dominance of big centers near the basket. There were other attempts to get even with USF, not all of them as equitable as the rule changes. Russell did not get the MVP award after the 1956 tournament, a gesture that seemed specifically designed to express a sense of resentment. (He was, however, chosen to the Olympic team, along with K.C. Jones; the U.S. took the Gold Medal easily, winning each of its eight games by at least 30 points.)

There was about the treatment of San Francisco one aspect which may have made a special impact on Russell. The team was largely black, and this seemed to bother a number of people. One San Francisco alumnus objected, "They are scarcely representative of the school. Perhaps a rule should be established that only three can be on the court at any one time."

By the time of the 1956 draft, Auerbach knew that Russell was the player who had the potential to make his team the defensive, fast-breaking team that would win a championship. But there were two problems. First, Boston did not have the first draft choice; the two teams with first crack were Rochester and St. Louis. Second, Abe Saperstein of the Harlem Globetrotters wanted Russell to play with his touring team, and was supposedly prepared to offer Russell an unheard-of amount of money to join his show—some $40,000. The second problem was solved rather quickly. Saperstein had an abiguous notion about race. On the one hand, he gave hundreds of black players a chance to play for money at a time when professional basketball was not hiring blacks. On the other hand, he seemed to regard Negroes as his personal property. He had threatened to refuse to play doubleheaders with the NBA when blacks started entering the league in 1950, apparently on the theory that he had exclusive rights to all basketball players with dark pigmentation. In any event, Saperstein sought to win Russell over by getting a black player to intercede for him, a play which—along with the year-round playing schedule of the Globies—was enough to turn Russell's attention to the NBA.

That left the draft to contend with. The Celtics' choice did not come until sixth. After finding that Rochester's Lester Harrison lacked the money to meet Russell's asking price of $25,000, Auerbach went to the next club on the draft list: Ben Kerner's St. Louis Hawks, the club Auerbach had coached years ago when they were known as the Tri-Cities Blackhawks. Kerner did not want to pay $25,000 for anybody, Russell included. Auerbach knew that Ed Macauley had a child who needed medical care in St. Louis, and that Macauley was even considering retirement just to get there. So Auerbach proposed sending Macauley to St. Louis for the rights to Russell. Kerner wanted more, and they agreed on Cliff Hagan, the Kentucky star whom Auerbach had drafted with his inventive use of the graduating class rule. Hagan was just completing his military service and had not yet played for Boston. The deal was made, and Russell joined Boston in November 1956, after playing in the Melbourne Olympics.

Russell came to the Celtics with a national reputation as a defensive player, but he was not yet a fully confident pro. He was a poor shooter—the worst in the NBA, as he remembers it. ("My favorite shot," he said in his first season, "is to hold the ball ten inches above the basket and then drop it through the hoop.") Auerbach was singularly unmoved by this weakness. "Who the hell wants a guy six-ten to shoot from beyond the foul line?" he asked. Ironically, Russell's defensive style of play was to make outside-shooting centers a valuable NBA commodity.

Moreover, Russell was receiving a rookie's typical NBA welcome: near the basket, he was being pulled, held, elbowed, pummeled and generally pounded by veterans who were making it clear that he would have to fight to hold and keep position at either end of the court. After six weeks, he was all but ready to quit.

Yet perhaps those first NBA appearances gave a clue as to what Russell could do once he learned the ropes. In his very first NBA game, against the St. Louis Hawks (who would be the principal rivals of the Celtics those first few years), Russell played twenty-one minutes and shot 3 for 11 from the floor and 0 for 4 from the free-throw line. But he also pulled down sixteen rebounds, and blocked three straight shots by Bob Pettit.

In his first game against the New York Knickerbockers, Russell was taken to the cleaners by Harry Gallatin at both ends of the court. The second time they met, in January 1957, Russell got six rebounds in the first five minutes and held Gallatin to 9 points, blocking four of his shots. (He had a horrible day on offense, hitting 1 for 10.)

By the end of his first season in the NBA, the Celtics had a division title and a league championship, both for the first time. For five years, they had been contenders, with superb shooters, aggressive defense, and a coach with a simple, winning theory. Now they had the man they had always lacked; the man to get them the ball, to trigger the break with the outlet pass, to make it possible for Boston to use its speed, Cousy's ball-handling and passing ability, Sharman's shot. It is no coincidence that the first time they fielded a top-flight rebounder (Russell was fourth in the league in his rookie season) they won it all.

Moreover, the presence of Russell made the other Celtics play the way Auerbach wanted the game played. They knew they had the center who could make the pieces fall into place. Each time the opposing team took a shot, the Celtics instinctively began to think transition, from defense to offense. It is an Auerbach axiom that the break begins on defense; with Russell, Boston was thinking of the move to offense as soon as the ball went into the air. Cousy would hover around the defensive key, the forwards would be ready to hit the side-lines, and a trailer, Sharman, would be ready to move down-court behind them for a possible open shot.

Russell had the capacity to quicken the transition, to catch the opposing team off-balance. A fast-break offense is not just a matter of hiring five sprinters to outrun the other team. It is a matter of moving downcourt *with the ball;* the re-bounder, in other words, must not simply get the ball; he must get it to his teammates if they mean to make it down-court ahead of the other team for any good purpose. Bill Russell had two methods of accomplishing this. The first was his capacity to throw the outlet pass while coming off a rebound. One of the criminal consequences of the scoring-oriented coverage of sports is that it turns attention away from other, infinitely less common skills. To watch Bill Rus-sell leap up, pull a missed shot out of the air, then turn and pass the ball off to a breaking Celtic, was to watch the fusion of intelligence and prowess that makes athletics worth watching. Of all the centers who have ever played the game, only Dave Cowens approaches Russell in his capacity to turn defense into offense so devastatingly, and only Wes Unseld and Wilt Chamberlain (in his later career) ever approached Russell in the art of throwing the outlet pass.

Russell's second tool for the conversion of defense into offense was revolutionary: the use of the blocked shot. He himself described this as "the biggest innovation that I helped bring about. . . . When I was a young man, the good coaches said that the good defensive players kept their feet on the floor. Well, you can't block shots with your feet on the floor."

Russell did not stay on the floor. His style was to use his exquisite sense of timing and his leaping ability (he high-jumped 6'7-1/2" in college) to prevent the ball from ever reaching the basket, and—more important—to guide the ball to another teammate. His sense of timing was so good that he was able to control the ball, to block it over to Cousy or Sam Jones or John Havlicek, and trigger the devastating fast break. A blocked shot is always a psychological blow to the opposing team; it puts a sudden, explosive end to their struggle for points. But when it results not merely in ending the rival's scoring hopes, but a score for the defending team, it becomes even more demoralizing. And this was Russell's unique skill.

Further, Russell's very presence made Auerbach's pressure defense that less risky. As one ex-Celtic remarked, "A guy like Russell can make a defensive hero out of a lot of stiffs." With a quick, smart, intimidating center like Russell protecting the basket, a guard can gamble much more on defense without suffering the consequences of a miss. If he steals the ball or disrupts the offense, fine; if not, there is always Russell waiting to dissuade the opposition from driving to the basket.

Finally, in listing the assets of Russell on the court, one must return to psychology. Twenty years ago, his coach at San Francisco, Phil Woolpert, said, "Much of [Russell's defensive value] is psychological—a shooter hurrying a shot he shouldn't take in order to avoid him."

Jerry West agreed. After his Lakers lost to the Celtics in the 1965 playoffs, he said, "You take the shot when you have it with Russell. You don't try to get any closer. The whole picture changes fast with him around."

Tom Hawkins of the Cincinnati Royals called it "Russell-phobia," explaining, "It's a thing that happens to people when they play the Celtics. I've seen guys going in for an uncontested lay-up—I mean, nobody near them—and just when they get up there, they suddenly look nervously over their shoulder for Russell to fall on them."

Of course, the fear of Russell usually had a good basis in reality. As Hawkins admitted, "I've gone in there and jumped a foot over the basket—which is quite a jump—and

I've looked up and there is Bill Russell a foot above *me,* about to stuff the ball down my throat." After a few experiences like that, the threat worked as well as the action itself. And like many of Russell's attributes, this is one that statistics can't measure.

Indeed, a novice looking at the numbers might puzzle over Russell's greatness. Not only did this center never lead the league in scoring, he never led his *team* in scoring; his career average was 15.1 points, and he never averaged 20 points a game in any season. He had a club lead for four straight seasons in field goal percentage, but that is explained mostly by the fact that he rarely took shots except from close in; he was a dreadful outside shot. He was also a dreadful foul shooter, averaging .561 over his career—although Jim Loscutoff claims that "Russell was the greatest shooter whenever you needed the points. If he was in a one-and-one situation and he was shooting the free throws, he'd always score those two points. The greatest pressure player I ever saw."

A glimpse across the Russell years, and some random judgments of his contemporaries, may offer a further example of just how remarkable Russell was.

•In 1960, in the seventh playoff game against St. Louis, Bob Pettit was so overwhelmed by Russell's defensive play that he said, just after a heartbreaking loss of a championship, "That man Russell is a credit to basketball. I think he played today what could be called one of the truly great games of all time."

•A year later, when the Celtics completed a 4–1 rout of the same Hawks, Russell played all forty-eight minutes, scoring 30 points and pulling down 38 rebounds—more than the five Hawk starters put together. As if to prove Loscutoff's point about his pressure shooting, Russell hit 9 for 17 from the floor, and 12 of 17 free throws.

•In the seventh game of the 1966 playoffs, Auerbach's last game as coach, Russell led the Celtics to a 95–93 squeaker, scoring 25 points, getting 32 rebounds, and blocking six shots. Throughout the seven games, he made 51 of 57 free throws.

•Near the end of his playing career, in February of 1969, Russell suffered acutely strained ligaments in his right knee, shortly before his thirty-fifth birthday. With Russell out, Boston lost five straight games—its longest losing streak in twenty years. So, in a game against the Philadelphia 76ers, Russell came back with a brace and a dragging leg. As Billy Cunningham, the once and present 76er remembers it: "The old man seemed to pump confidence into them, as though they were saying to themselves, 'Now we can come back and win.' " Cunningham recalls how Russell stood at the foul line, mumbling, "I have this pain in my legs, it shoots all the way down to my toes," just before grabbing a teammate's missed foul shot and dunking it. Playing on one and a half legs, Russell grabbed 23 rebounds, and on the last play of regulation time sprinted ahead of the field to tie the game with a stuff. Boston won it in overtime.

Off and on the court, Russell was always the psychologist, always looking for a special edge. If he ran into a rival at a restaurant the night before the game, he would snub him, hoping to get his man so steamed up that he would be concentrating the next night on bothering Russell instead of fitting in with his team. Russell would mutter to opponents that they were not getting their fair share of shots. He would pick and choose his moments of shot-blocking. If he was lucky, he once explained, he could block 8 to 10 percent of the shots taken against him. The secret was in knowing which 8 or 10 percent—which shots, when blocked, would so demoralize an opponent that he would be off his game for the rest of the night.

But Russell's most remarkable feat of psychology was his own capacity to concentrate on the basketball court while his life off the court was an endless series of conflicts and contro-

versies. In a sense, Russell seems to have decided—early on
—that he would have to survive off the court the same way
he survived on it, by clearing out a space for himself with
flailing arms and legs, by making it clear that nobody was
going to crowd Bill Russell. One of the people who worked
with him long after his playing days remembers Russell saying, "We spend our lives building walls around us, and then
hope someone will come along to tear them down." For
Russell, that wall was built of the twin pressures of celebrity-
hood and racial conflict. That sometimes led to conduct that
was disagreeable, even repugnant. But it cannot be understood without placing Russell in the context of his time and
place.

Russell was six-nine, and a national celebrity, but neither
of those facts immunized him from the routine treatment of
American blacks. In 1962, he and his family drove through
the South to visit his grandfather in Louisiana. With a carful
of children crying for food and rest, Russell had to drive on
and on through the night, unable to find a place where he
could be served food or given a place to sleep for himself and
his family. That same year (and earlier, and later), hotels in
Kentucky and the Carolinas and the Virginias would not
serve Russell and the other black members of the Celtic
team. He went to Jackson, Mississippi, in the "Freedom
Summer" of 1964 at the request of Charles Evers to give
basketball clinics—integrated—and found his life threatened
in a Mississippi 'restaurant.

And this happened not simply in the South. At his first
press conference after being named coach of the Celtics in
1966, Russell was asked if he would be able to judge white
players on the basis of their abilities. It is not recorded that
the same question, with the colors reversed, was ever asked
of a white coach about his black players.

Moreover, Russell was playing in a city whose reputation
and reality are not always coterminous. To many, Boston is

the symbol of liberty, the cradle of the American Revolution, the intellectual center for abolitionists like William Lloyd Garrison and Charles Sumner. True; but Boston is also a hotbed of ethnic and class divisions. Like every big city in the Northeast, Boston is filled with the descendants of the immigrant waves, competing with each other, and with the settled establishment, for money, jobs, turf and power. Boston has seen decades of this sort of struggle: the Yankees against the Irish, against the Italian, against the Jewish (investigative reporter John Roy Carlson called Boston during World War II "the most anti-Semitic city in America"). The city did not experience a major black influx until after the War, and by the mid-1950's racial tension was already a fact of life. (This kind of double-identity is still very much with Boston; it is the capital, and principal city, of the only state to vote for George McGovern over Richard Nixon in 1972, yet it is the scene of some of the most violent racial hostility, sparked by busing but actually running much deeper.)

When Russell joined the Celtics, and led them to the team's first title in 1957, attendance leaped to the 10,000 mark and the Celtic future looked good. But that was the last year the Celtics would ever see that kind of attendance figure until the dynasty years were over and the team began its climb back toward contention. Inexplicably, the perennial champions averaged attendances of 8,000, 7,500, 6,500, in an arena which could hold 15,320. And throughout those years, the Boston Bruins, with a cellar-dwelling record to match that of a Manhattan cockroach, filled the same arena almost every night they played.

There were a welter of reasons. Apart from the realities of geography and climate, which made hockey a more naturally favored sport in the region, Boston's one group of potential basketball fans found the Celtics inaccessible. The college-educated professionals, who had learned something of the sport in college, lived outside the city, in the suburbs beyond

Route 128. Going to see the Celtics meant a long journey into what may charitably be described as a "working class" neighborhood, with all the discomforts and dangers of crowded streets, inadequate parking and grimy surroundings that can unsettle the comfortable. The Garden was easily within reach by mass transportation from other parts of the city, but Boston's working people, radically different from New York's, had no tie at all with basketball. It was not the playground ritual; it had no evocation of childhood or neighborhood prowess; it had no capacity to bind them to the sport year after year. Some of the obsession with sports comes from a sharp re-creation of the past; the Celtics were deprived of that benefit.

It has to be understood that mass spectator sports are in general the pleasure of the less affluent groups. To be rich means access to beaches, tennis courts, stables, golf courses, country clubs, the sense of personal use of great stretches of land. To be poor, or to be getting by, means a life spent in crowds—on public beaches, on mass transportation, on lines, in movie theaters and sports arenas. There are occasional quirks, of course: the New York Knicks and Los Angeles Lakers have both been taken up at times by the well-heeled and the well-known. But by and large, at least in the cities of the Northeast, the great arenas are the pleasure palaces of the not-very-well-off. It is exactly those groups which, from Boston to Detroit, have rubbed up most closely against racial frictions—fights over jobs and neighborhoods and resources.

In Dan Jenkins' very funny novel *Semi-Tough,* a friend of Southern football star Billy Clyde Puckett defines pro basketball: "Ever' 24 seconds, ten niggers jump up in the air." And that sentiment was not confined to fictional Southern football players. There were plenty of sports fans who did not like the look of a home team with as many black athletes as Boston had, particularly after Sam and K.C. Jones replaced Cousy and Sharman, and Tom Sanders took up a forward position.

The name "Celtics" had been picked partially in homage to the old Original Celtics, but also to reflect the Irish base in Boston. And for some fans, a black man could not reflect the sense of a tie, however tenuous, with Irish blood. It requires no sociological study to see that a group feeling threatened by racial conflict will find it hard to develop a rooting interest in a team whose members seem to be drawn from the ranks of the "enemy."

Russell's response to this climate would be unremarkable today. He was angry about it and open about his anger. "There are two societies in this country," he said, three years before the Kerner Commission Report, "and I have to recognize it . . . to see life for what it is . . . not to go stark raving mad." Neither the time nor the place was ready for that kind of bluntness. It was a time, remember, when athletes were considered autistic demigods, blessed of body, weak of mind. Sports reporters described a player's exploits in Homeric terms but reduced the athlete himself to a mumbler of homilies. When the press and public encountered a tall, black, blunt athlete with strong opinions on explosive matters, they went into culture shock. As early as 1958, Russell told *Sports Illustrated,* "I don't like most white people because they are white. Conversely, I like most Negroes because they are black." He later modified his philosophy, saying it wasn't necessary to be anti-white in order to be pro-black, but the earlier sentiments remained a part of Russell's persona. This impression, that the heart and soul of the Celtic team was anti-white, threw out of focus most of Russell's words and deeds about race—words and deeds which seem so unexceptionable today.

He attacked basketball in a notorious piece in *Sports Illustrated* for maintaining a quota system under which only two or three blacks played on the floor for any one team at any one time. The truth of that statement was as obvious—literally—as black and white. Even now, white athletes are con-

sidered more attractive attendance boosters than black athletes in most cities. The market value of an Ernie deGregorio,
as against a black six-foot guard of comparable ability, is a
prime example of a "great white hope" mentality that is still
with us today. Indeed, when the Celtics got Willie Naulls in
1963, one Boston columnist wrote that the team could not use
him because it was already too black (with Russell, Tom
Sanders and the Joneses). If Russell had a sense that there
was resistance to full black participation in basketball, as
well the rest of society, he had more than his share of evidence.

Moreover, Russell's personality was singularly ill-suited to
the consequences of fame. The oldest cliché of the star syn-
drome is the poor, struggling actor (or dancer, or ballplayer)
who climbs to the top, only to find that life at the top is not
what it seems. The very elements that bring big salaries and
national recognition also bring with them a status which
strips away the comfortable distance between star and fan.

For Russell, the combination of the fans' lust for contact
with him and their racial rejection of him was intolerable.
His famous refusal to sign autographs was based on many
different reasonings—that a signature on a scrap of paper
had any meaning, for example. But one ex-Celtic said, "I
always figured Bill believed he was signing autographs for
kids whose parents didn't want his kids to go to school with
their kids. He just didn't want to play any games like that."

Whatever the reason, Russell and Boston did not develop
a warm, personal relationship. He was to say, after taking the
job as Seattle's coach and general manager, "I did not enjoy
Boston. I enjoyed playing with the Celtics. I enjoyed the
other players. I did not enjoy living there." And he also,
publicly, called Boston "the most rigidly segregated city in
America," and claimed that sportswriters were among the
most prejudiced people he knew. "When I went there," he
said of Boston, "I felt they had a code of conduct first for

athletes, and another for black athletes."

Many of the writers returned the compliment. Russell had come to Boston at a time when a single basketball hero had dominated the community for almost a decade—Bob Cousy. And that affection may have tinged the writers' perceptions of what was happening on the court. "When he came here," P.R. man Howie McHugh says, "everybody here talked of nothing but Cousy . . . We'd go into the dressing room after Russell had won the game, and the press would all flock to Cousy, and Russell would be sitting there in the corner, the guy who won the game, and nobody would say anything."

As his public aloofness grew, so did resentment. After his first year as coach, writer Al Hirshberg devoted a column to Russell's rudeness, and then filled another one with letters supporting his stand. One black man wrote, "I took my 19 year old son to [dinner], when Russell came in, dressed in his cape. When my son held out his hand, Russell not only refused to take it, but pushed the boy to one side, almost knocking him over." Hirshberg said, "If Russell will not or cannot accept those responsibilities [to be civil], then he should resign as coach of the Celtics. And if he won't resign, Red Auerbach, who appointed him, should fire him."

After Russell's comment about Boston from Seattle, the *Herald*'s Tim Horgan wrote of him: "He was the most surly, selfish, and uncooperative athlete I've met in 23 years as a Boston sportswriter." Nor did the Celtic star ever make any secret of his feelings. In a famous *Saturday Evening Post* article in 1964, entitled "I Owe the Public Nothing," he said, "I'm not going to smile if I don't feel like smiling, and bow my head modestly. Because it's not my nature . . . I don't think it's incumbent upon me to set a good example for anybody's kids but my own."

The storms inside Russell were a startling contrast to his combination of composure, grace and exertion on the court. There are photographs that catch him in a moment of utter extension, and the contrast between his serene face and his fully extended body is remarkable. At such times he looked like a classic dancer: arm totally stretched in a straight line from his body, ankles crossed, face emotionless. Even here, however, appearances are deceiving. Russell's cackling laugh and low-key locker room remarks were a steadying influence on his teams for years. But he also vomited before any important game. His teammates used to listen for the sound of his retching as a reassuring sign that Russell was up for the game.

As a private person, Russell showed signs of depression as well as anger. He often prophesied that he would die early. He believed that the law of averages would someday catch up with him in an airplane, that he would die in a crash. And one reporter who interviewed Russell at thirty-two—the age at which his mother died—found him haunted by the specter of death. His wife at the time remembered his concern over unintentionally wounding a friend: "I'll be glad when I die," he said, "and then I'll be alone and I won't hurt anyone again." Or he would justify his travels and hectic life by rationalizing that "I'll get all this and retire young and then I won't have to worry about dying."

He was as harsh a critic of his own life as he was of others'. "Until today," he told writer Milton Gross in 1962, "my life has been a waste. What does this all mean? This is without depth . . . I feel that playing basketball is just marking time. I don't feel that this can be it for a man. I haven't accomplished anything, really." If he had it to do again, he said, "I guess I would try to be a doctor, or engineer, or architect."

His words were a grim echo of the old Groucho Marx quip: "I would never join any club that would have me as a member." He was earning $200,000 a year when he quit the Celtics as a player-coach, yet even then his extraordinary skills were devoted to what he considered a shallow and superficial enterprise.

This may account for Russell's consistent refusal to celebrate himself in the pageantry of sport. He was the only member of the NBA Silver Anniversary Team who did not appear in San Diego for the ceremonies in 1971. When his old number 6 was added to the Boston Garden rafters in March of 1972, he only participated on condition the ceremony be held before the doors of the Garden opened to the crowd. And in 1975 he refused to attend his induction ceremony at the Basketball Hall of Fame.

The years following Russell's retirement, however, saw an odd shift in his relations with the public. He still refused to back away from controversy, but the barrier between himself and the public seemed to recede. His personality became an increasingly attractive commodity. Whether because the times had changed, or because his candor was a refreshing contrast to the prepackaged plastic of most sports figures, Russell found himself a popular public figure, and ultimately he carved out a new career in the shallow and empty sport that he dominated as has no other single player before or since.

8

Wilt Chamberlain: The Anti-Celtic

Victory is the essence of success in sports, but it can some-times produce a backlash. Since controversy is almost as much fun as watching games—writers need something to do on road trips, and citizens confused about economics or legislation feel fully informed about their favorite sports—there are always people ready to demonstrate that a cham-pionship team was the beneficiary of blind luck, of shadowy help from the officials, or of an unfair amount of wealth. A team that always wins is rarely universally admired; there are too many disappointed fans in other cities, and sometimes even home fans can get bored with annual pennants.

The Boston Celtics had one special asset, one amulet that helped keep pro basketball audiences generally appreciative. He never scored a point for Boston; he never played one minute with Boston; indeed, he spent his life on opposite teams. His name was Wilt Chamberlain. For a decade, he played against the Celtic teams of the dynasty years. For nine of the ten years when Russell's teams entered the playoffs, they faced a team anchored by one of the two or three most awesome players in the history of basketball. Twice they faced a West Coast Chamberlain team for the championship; seven times they battled him as a member of a Philadelphia team for the Eastern final, in what was usually regarded as the "real" championship. In most of these contests, Boston was regarded as an underdog, or at best an even shot, despite the clear evidence that the Celtics were putting on the floor the best collection of basketball brains and talent ever assembled. Each year, instead of boredom setting in among basketball observers and writers as this steamroller flattened the competition, a new chapter was opened in what became an enduring sports-entertainment myth: "Can Boston Stop Wilt?" It is not too much to say that Auerbach and the Celtic alumni owe a fervent prayer of thanks to Wilt Chamberlain: his presence was the backdrop against which the achievements of Boston grew to legend.

To those whose interest in basketball is casual, the big man is a symbol of the limits of the sport. If I were eight feet tall, people say, I could be a basketball star, too. Just give me the ball, I'll walk up to the basket and drop it in. The history of basketball shows just how false this perception is. Of the hundreds of big men who entered the ranks of the National Basketball Association before 1970, only two players seven feet tall or more are likely to be remembered as exceptional: Wilt Chamberlain and Kareem Abdul-Jabbar. For every great big man, there are a dozen Walter Dukeses or Henry Finkels, men who simply lack the athletic skills to stay with their opponents and their teammates. The game cannot be played by stalking around the court, looming over players. Mobility, hand-eye coordination, anticipation, quickness, reflexes and a fair share of brains are essential parts of the game. And there are not that many seven-foot tall people who possess these athletic skills.

Through the first decade of professional basketball, only

one "giant," six-ten George Mikan of the Minneapolis Lakers, proved himself to be an authentic superstar. Mikan played the pivot, taking the ball from playmaking guards like Slater Martin and Whitey Skoog, and passing to the cutters or to open forwards. In addition, he had a fine hook shot, a good outside shot, rebounding smarts, and a first-rate basketball ability wrapped up in a very tall frame. In 1956, Bill Russell put his six-nine height to work primarily as a rebounder and a defensive genius, combining that height (which some people insisted had to be seven feet plus) with remarkable anticipation and agility. Had Bill Russell been permitted to occupy the basketball ozone by himself, much of the Celtic dynasty would have been dismissed with a shrug of the shoulders and the easy explanation that of *course* Boston won, because they had the best big man ever to play the game. But with the coming of Wilt, things changed.

Wilt Chamberlain became famous when he was still playing for Overbrook High School in Philadelphia. Unlike Russell, who says he did not begin really growing until he was sixteen, Chamberlain was an early riser: six-foot-three by the time he was twelve, six-seven when he was in junior high school. But more important, Chamberlain was a gifted natural athlete. He was a track star in high school and college, setting a Big Eight freshman high jump record his first year at the University of Kansas, and later jumping seven feet. He was fast, enormously strong, and coordinated. While still in high school, his picture was in *Life* magazine, and one sports publication tabbed him as ready to play in the pros without any college basketball at all.

His two varsity years at Kansas were impressive but frustrating. In his sophomore year, he led the Big Eight in scoring with a 25.4 average, and Kansas won the conference championship easily, with an overall 24-3 record. But in the NCAA championships, North Carolina beat Kansas by one point in triple overtime. In Chamberlain's junior year, despite a 28.3 scoring average, a rash of injuries cost Kansas the conference championship. Wilt dropped out of school to tour with the Harlem Globetrotters for a year until his college class graduated and he could play for the Philadelphia Warriors, who had territorial draft rights to him.

Chamberlain, to some sports people, represented the embodiment of all of their fears about the "big man" role. In fact, a struggling young sportswriter named Jimmy Breslin wrote a magazine piece asking, "Can Basketball Survive Chamberlain?" before Wilt had ever played a professional game. The assumption was that his height, combined with his skills, would virtually end NBA competition; that Chamberlain could take any team and propel it to victory. Even knowledgeable basketball people had jumped to the same conclusion: Phog Allen, the man who had recruited Chamberlain to Kansas, proclaimed, "With him, we'll never lose a game; we could win the national championship with Wilt, two sorority girls, and two Phi Beta Kappas."

Such statements build up ridiculous expectations and make any defeat of the media-hyped superman's team an event of historic proportions. They also inevitably cast the team that beats such a Goliath into heroes, Davids, giant-killers.

And the Russell-led Celtics proceeded to spend the next ten years playing that role.

From the first time they met, the media machine (sports division) advertised "the Battle of the Titans," "the Battle of the Giants," or whatever catch-phrase a clever public relations man could sell. On November 7, 1959, the Warriors came into Boston Garden for Chamberlain's first meeting with Russell and the Celtics, and the Boston Garden had championship hysteria. No, that's not quite right. The Celtics in those days rarely sold out any game, including the championships. But for the first Russell-Chamberlain duel, scalpers were asking $10 a ticket (in a day when regular-season tickets at Boston Garden could be had for $2.50). When the dust cleared, Chamberlain had outscored Russell, 30–22; Russell had out-rebounded Chamberlain, 35–28; and Boston had beaten Philadelphia, 115–106. Chamberlain's height and reputation (and his salary, the highest in NBA history) had erased his "rookie" status. Instead, the press went berserk because Russell had blocked a Chamberlain shot, as if it had never happened to Wilt before. Suddenly, Russell had become the scrappy little guy—at least when he faced Chamberlain.

The first season presaged what was to come. Chamberlain broke every record in the book, from points scored to game average to minutes played, and he took Russell's rebounding crown away from him. He was named Rookie of the Year and Most Valuable Player—the first time for that to happen in any major sport. But the Celtics finished first in the Eastern Division, then beat the Warriors in six games for the division playoff title (Tom Heinsohn tipped in a winning basket in the sixth game). Then they beat the St. Louis Hawks in seven games for the NBA championship. Year after year, Chamberlain would lead his teams to the playoffs, only to find defeat at the hands of the Celtics. Three times Wilt moved across the continent—from Philadelphia to San Francisco with the Warriors, back to Philadelphia to play with the 76ers, then to Los Angeles to play with the Lakers. And every time but one—in 1967, when the 76ers finished far ahead of the Celtics with a 68-13 record, then wiped them out in five playoff games—Chamberlain's teams came out second best in their struggles against the Celtics.

The pattern varied. Sometimes the contest went down to the last minute. In the famous 1965 seventh game, Philadelphia, trailing by one point, got the ball with five seconds left because Russell's in-bounds pass hit a guy wire. Then Havlicek stole Philadelphia's in-bounds pass to save the game and the series for Boston. In the seventh game of the finals in 1969, with Chamberlain on the bench after a painful knee injury, Boston squeaked to a 108–106 victory and the dynasty team's last championship. Other times, Boston won more easily—in a five-game rout of the Warriors in 1964, in another five-game battering of the 76ers in 1966. But the persistent success of the Celtics over Chamberlain gave rise to more theories than the anatomical location of the female orgasm.

Some people argued that Russell had Chamberlain "psyched." Others, Chamberlain most prominently, argued that Boston had a better team and better coaching—that no one man, however good, could be expected to carry his team to victory. Whatever the reason, the Celtics' ability to dominate the most awesome individual offensive threat in basketball was proof for Red Auerbach that his own theory was sound.

Auerbach took every opportunity to argue for the superiority of Russell. When Chamberlain was a high school player spending summers at Kutsher's Country Club (and Russell not yet in Boston), Auerbach had suggested Wilt attempt to enter Harvard—which would have meant that Chamberlain could become a territorial draft pick of the Celtics. But as the years went on, Auerbach made a point of denigrating Chamberlain, comparing him unfavorably with Russell, and asking how many championships Chamberlain's teams had won. The bad feeling grew to the point that Chamberlain refused to play in the Maurice Stokes Charity Games at Kutsher's Country Club unless he had a chance to beat a team coached by Auerbach.

Near the end of Chamberlain's rookie year, for example, Auerbach declared that Russell was more valuable to his team than Wilt could ever be. "The Celtics are a running ball club," he said, "and Russell fits in better with our style of play—better than Chamberlain would. I'll concede that Wilt

is the better scorer, but do you think the Celtic scoring
average would be any greater if Chamberlain was playing for
us? Well, let me assure you, it wouldn't."

And in Chamberlain's second year in the league, when he
was breaking all of his own scoring records, Auerbach began
growling about the overemphasis on Wilt. When Russell
took the MVP award, his coach gloated, "For the past four
and a half months, all [the NBA] sent out was Chamberlain,
Chamberlain, Chamberlain, like he was on the NBA payroll.
We were running away from Chamberlain's team in the
standings, and from the publicity they sent out you'd never
know the Celtics were in the league, or that Russell was on
the Celtics."

Wilt, Auerbach said in 1961, wasn't the most valuable
player in the league, nor even the second. Auerbach rated
him about fifth—behind Russell, Bob Pettit of the Hawks,
Elgin Baylor of the Lakers, and Oscar Robertson of the
Royals. "To read NBA press releases," he added pointedly,
"you'd never suspect there was such a thing as defensive
ability in the league. Offense, offense, offense, that's all they
write about."

It may be that this was just another part of Auerbach's
psychological warfare, designed to infuriate the big center
and convince the Celtics that the fight to beat Chamberlain
was a matter of principle. But there was also something very
close to basic basketball principle that might have made
Auerbach so critical.

Chamberlain, and the individual dominance he represented, was as much a threat to Auerbach's commitment to
team play and balanced scoring as Russell was an embodiment of that commitment. He might as well have been speaking of Chamberlain when he said, "The only true statistics
are the foul shooting figures, which everyone can see and
count. The rest is garbage. Give me a ball club—like the
Celtics—where everyone is in double figures almost every

game, and with no one man dominating the scoring."

This was precisely the same point Auerbach had made when he was coaching the old Washington Capitals; it was a matter of the right way to play and to win basketball, and Chamberlain was a threat to that theory and practice.

Oddly, Russell himself maintained a respectful public attitude toward his rival. "I'll never forget the first time we both got our hands on the same rebound, and I tried to take the ball away from him," he said after Wilt's second season. "I've got good, strong hands, but Wilt just picked up me and the ball together. I was hoping he wouldn't try a dunk shot. I could have been in real trouble going through the basket."

Russell and Chamberlain laughed at the attempts to build their professional rivalry into a personal feud. But after Chamberlain's one clear-cut triumph over Russell and the Celtics in 1967, Wilt said the Boston team had been outcoached—and the coach that year happened to be Bill Russell. Then, after his retirement, Russell claimed that Chamberlain had copped out in the 1969 championship game when he took himself out with a knee injury. After that blast, relations between the two were cool—or perhaps nonexistent.

Debating the relative merits among sports figures is as valuable as deciding who George McGovern would have put in his cabinet. But the evidence supplied by Chamberlain himself strongly suggests that Russell, or the Russell style of play, may simply have been a smarter use of a dominant big man. In 1967, the year the 76ers took the title away from Boston after eight straight Celtic triumphs, Chamberlain played on a team with a style that seemed a brilliant copy of the Celtic success formula. There were, he tells us, no cliques, none of the black-white divisions that had marked other teams he had played on. Wilt took half as many shots as usual (1,150, almost exactly Russell's average). His scoring average dropped to 24 points a game, but four 76ers were among the league's top fifteen scorers. And Chamberlain finished third in the league in assists that year.

Then, in 1972, Chamberlain played for Laker coaches Bill Sharman and K.C. Jones—two ex-Celtics—and became a sensational fast-break-oriented center. The Lakers won thirty-three straight games (an all-time major league sports record), won more regular-season games than any team in NBA history, and won the playoff finals in five games from New York. Their defense-oriented, rebounding center, who threw the outlet pass, rested (if at all) on offense, and frequently shot less than a dozen times a game, was the "new" Wilt Chamberlain.

As Chamberlain himself said, a very tall, brilliantly gifted basketball player not only mobilizes his opponents (who want to be giant-killers), but lulls his own team into a sense of false security. They may move less without the ball because he can score so easily from in close; they may work a little less hard on getting open, on creating screens, on boxing out, because the Big Man is there to do it for them.

In a way, Russell's road was easier because he was less talented on offense. In any case, given the strong egos on the Celtics, there was less danger of Boston's teams relying too heavily on him. They knew full well that they would have to compensate for his offensive weakness, just as he would compensate for their defensive limitations.

Chamberlain, by contrast, was so talented that he may well have deprived his teammates of those elements of will and concentration that make the difference in critical moments of critical games. And yet he may have helped to create a dynasty despite the records of his own teams. His presence in the NBA throughout the Celtics' victory years always gave Boston a dragon to slay. Even when they piled title upon title, there was always Wilt to pose a seemingly unmoveable barrier between them and the next title. He was the credible, feared opponent that makes victory a challenge instead of a routine. By his talent, then, Chamberlain became both a contrast and a worthy rival: the anti-Celtic who helped to define the team, and to provide a measure of its achievement.

9

Sam and K.C. Jones: Continuity

Building a championship team requires talent, motivation, intelligence and luck. The irrational nature of blind luck, if nothing else, usually assures that championship play does not often settle into a town for a long run. The draft, in a five-man sport, can quickly turn a wretched basketball team into a contender (witness the Milwaukee Bucks after the arrival of Abdul-Jabbar in 1971). The incapacitation of one man can remove the keystone of a winning team (witness the New York Knicks after Willis Reed's legs gave out). The odds against repeating as champions are greater in basketball than in other sports because, as Bob Cousy puts it, "Basketball is *the* pure team sport." Every element in every position must work: the playmaking guard, the shooting guard, the quick forward, the power forward, the center.

If there is one fundamental lesson to be learned from the astonishing thirteen-year reign of the Boston Celtics, it is that a team wins when players are permitted to concentrate on their skills and to forget about their weaknesses. Let the defensive specialists harass the opponents' best ball handlers and shooters, and reward them for what they do well. Let the writers and fans bemoan the low statistical product. Tell your shooters to shoot, and not to worry about being called the "gunner." Tell your rebounding specialists not to brood about the inconsistent quality of their outside shooting. In other words, look at the game of basketball as a series of necessary skills that can be scattered among your team—as long as one player possesses an essential skill in extremely high quality.

The Celtics seemed at times to be less a collection of individuals than a collection of skills. Names and faces changed, but the quality of performance in each of the key skills of the game remained astonishingly high. The most enduring cliché of Celtic admirers is that Red Auerbach had a master's touch in getting the most out of his players, that he was a coaching genius not in the technical capacity of the game, but in the way he handled players. And he was known to choose them for reasons not directly related to their particular skills, selecting players who were part of championship teams, for example. But Auerbach's real talent may well have been his ability to see beyond the individual, to the specific skill he represented.

The conventional image of basketball, particularly as it is played in the inner city by urban blacks, is that of an ego sport, a game in which a youth deprived of many other sources of gratification finds his one chance to prove himself. In this sense, the Celtics were never a city team, nor did they play what has come to be known as "black" basketball, no matter what the color of the players on the court. (Yet in the mid-1960's, Boston became the first NBA team to break the unspoken taboo and field five black players on the court at the same time.) There was a consistent subordination of the ego to the job that needed doing, a studied lack of flamboyance for its own sake. Auerbach's emphasis on the team came from earlier generations of basketball and seemed to fly in the face of the school of play exemplified by Pete Maravich, Julius Erving and other crowd-pleasers. But his philosophy did not make the search for continuity easier.

When Boston finally won its first championship in 1957, continuity was not yet a major concern. Russell was a rookie; so was Tommy Heinsohn. Jim Loscutoff was twenty-seven; Frank Ramsey was twenty-five. The Celtic backcourt, for years the best in pro basketball, was a few years older: Bob Cousy, "Mr. Basketball," was twenty-eight; Bill Sharman, the best shooter, was thirty. Their careers were by no means over, but in contrast to Russell, who played forty-five or forty-eight minutes a night routinely, they could not be expected to play Boston's running style of basketball without relief. It was clear that the Celtic backcourt would be the first component of the team to need help. The way in which Auerbach found help goes far toward explaining his ability to create the greatest dynasty in sports history. From the perspective of fifteen years, it is still almost incredible to realize that at the start of the 1960's Boston had a pair of backcourt benchwarmers named Sam and K.C. Jones.

•

Sam Jones never thought he possessed enough basketball talent to play with Boston. Unlike players who attract national publicity at schools such as Indiana, Notre Dame and UCLA, and whose professional careers are charted long before they graduate, Sam Jones played out his amateur career in obscurity. Born to a desperately poor family, picking up cash in such diverse jobs as room-service waiter in Atlantic City and steelworker in Gary, Indiana, Jones went to all-black North Carolina College in the days when segregation was still the law in the South. He led his team to a 21-6 record, but they played far from the spotlight of post-season tournaments, television and big-city arenas. The Minneapolis Lakers considered drafting him, but decided there was simply no way to judge his ability because of the low caliber of his competition.

Once again, one of the Celtics' most consistent resources came to Auerbach's aid—his former associates. Bill Reinhart had flagged Bill Russell, and Bones McKinney (who played for Auerbach in Washington and Boston) had alerted him to Bill Sharman. Now, as the 1957 draft was about to begin, McKinney, serving as chaplain of Wake Forest University, called again. "Red," he said, "there's a colored kid down here with the damnedest bank shot you ever saw."

Having just won the NBA title with the best record in the league, Auerbach had the last draft rights. As he explained years later, "Sam was an unknown boy from an unknown school. But we had last draft choice, and I figured, Why not? There's nobody else left." Sam Jones became Boston's first round pick—and he was disappointed.

"I didn't want to play," Jones recalls, "not with the Celtics. I didn't think I'd make the team." Perhaps it was this uncertainty that gave him the expression with which he was tagged throughout his early career. Just as every baseball player named Simpson is called "Suitcase" (after the original, much-traded Harry Simpson), most athletes named Sam are labeled "Sad Sam," and Jones inherited that nickname. In Jones's case, however, the nickname was an understatement: his facial expression when he played was so woebegone that the first time he checked into an NBA game a courtside official asked solicitously, "Did someone die?" By the time Jones's twelve-year career was over, the answer was more often than not, Yes—the opposition.

For his first three years in the league, Sam Jones spent more time on the bench than on the floor, never averaging more than eighteen minutes a game, and never scoring for more than a 12-point average. But to Auerbach, as always, statistics were less important than the final scores. The fact is that, especially after Sam's namesake, K.C., came on board, Boston had a whole combination of backcourts that made it all but impossible for opponents to shut the Celtics down. For sheer experience, nothing could match Cousy and Sharman. For defensive pressure to hold a shrinking lead, Cousy and K.C. Jones were the mix. For firepower on a long, uphill comeback, Sharman and Sam. And for speed, the Jones Boys. It was a backcourt mix that for talent will probably never be equaled on any one NBA club.

Even before Sam and K.C. Jones became the starting backcourt of the Celtics, Auerbach knew he had something special. "I began to notice," he said, "that whenever they went into a game, if we were behind, we'd begin to catch up —and if we were ahead, we'd stay ahead. Meanwhile, Cousy and Sharman were getting a rest."

The essence of Sam Jones's value was offense. A forward while at college, the six-four Jones was a prototype of the big guard that dominates the NBA today. His size and strength enabled him both to shoot over smaller guards and to muscle his way into position for an open shot. "Sam is the best shooter in the NBA," Frank Ramsey said midway through Jones's career. "I've never seen another player who can get himself into good shooting position as fast as he."

In addition, Jones's shooting weapon was unorthodox: a bank shot. "Sam Jones used the backboard the way a pool shooter uses a cushion," the saying went. Frequently, opponents would give him a shot because it was from an "impossible" angle—but if the shooter was aiming off the glass instead of directly at the rim, the impossible angle turned into 2 points.

Many of those shots became the difference between victory and defeat for the Celtics. In 1958, in the finals against St. Louis, the rookie Jones came in for Heinsohn in the second game and scored 16 points in nineteen minutes to spark

Boston to a victory. In the seventh game of the 1960 championship game against the same Hawks, Jones hit 12 points in the second period as the Celtics tore the game open for a 122–103 win. In 1962, in the seventh game of the Eastern finals against Philadelphia, Jones's last-second jump shot won it for the Celtics, 109–107. The next year, against Cincinnati, again in a seventh-game situation, Jones hit for 47 points to wrap up the division for Boston. In beating the New York Knicks in the Eastern semifinals in 1967, Jones scored an incredible 51 points, a club record. His playoff farewell against the Los Angeles Lakers included one of his most bizarre shots ever. Trailing 2–1 in games, the Lakers held a 1-point lead with seconds left. Jones tossed up a stumbling, thirty-five-foot one-handed shot. He said later that he was hoping Russell could put in the rebound, but Russell had taken himself out of the game moments before. The crazy shot went in by itself, and the Celtics had the game.

Jones wound up his career with 15,344 points: he ranks behind Bob Cousy and John Havlicek among club scoring leaders. Perhaps more surprising, Jones, a guard who shot from the perimeter, had the highest shooting percentage on the team for six straight years—higher even than Russell, a center who rarely shot from further out than five feet.

Perhaps sportswriter Jim Murray described Sam Jones most accurately when he wrote that "the Celtics always keep one player around as a sort of transfusion specialist . . . Sam Jones did it for ten years. Whenever the Celtics were nine points down, it was Sam Jones' job to tie the score."

•

Ironically, Sam Jones is remembered best not for individual exploits, but as one-half of the "Jones Boys." The other half of the duo, K.C. Jones, was a different breed of player altogether. Their playing styles and talents were almost diametrically opposed. If there was any justice in their being yoked together in the public mind, it was that they complemented each other so perfectly.

With Bill Russell in the middle, other teams could not rely on the close-in shot, the lay-up, the penetration of a quick guard. There was one weapon, however, that a Russell beneath the basket did not cover: a sharp, outside shooter. If the opposition backcourt had accurate firepower from beyond the foul line, it could neutralize the defensive power of Russell, ultimately forcing the big man to come outside, thus opening up the middle for back-door plays and penetrating guards. What the Celtics needed to deny this possibility was a guard who could pressure the offensive backcourt, forcing the guards out of their rhythms, and the ball out of the backcourt and into traffic.

Sam Jones was a scorer, not a defensive guard. Defense was the job and the achievement of the second "new" guard, K.C. Jones. He was the first player in the history of the National Basketball Association ever to win his job solely on the basis of his defensive ability.

In his nine seasons with the Celtics, K.C. Jones scored only 4,999 points. He averaged 7.4 points per game, and in no season was his average higher than 9.1. He took fewer than 5,000 shots from the floor—a total exceeded every three years by Tom Heinsohn. But in eight of those nine years, K.C. Jones played on an NBA title team. His number hangs from the rafters of Boston Garden not because of the points he put into the basket, but because of the points he kept out. Jerry West said of him, "He's only the best defensive man in the league. Only the best." And his friend and college roommate, Bill Russell, not given to outbursts of enthusiasm, said, "I've never had a better friend or a greater inspiration. Over the years, I've seen K.C. do superhuman things and make them look natural. He's just plainly a superior person in and out of sports."

This performance was accompanied by a typical Celtic quality of quiet determination. Off the court, K.C. was something of an entertainer. Yet he played without apparent emotion, dazzling the crowd not with moves and spectacular ballet, but with a terrier-like determination to keep the opponent away from the basket. Coupled with Sam Jones's shooting skill, the quiet perseverance of K.C. gave the Celtics another generation of backcourt supremacy without which the dynasty would never have happened.

K.C. Jones was born in Dallas, Texas, and as a child moved with his mother to San Francisco. He was a natural athlete, playing football, baseball and basketball. Like Bill Russell, he was a late grower—he was sixteen before he was taller than most of his companions—and he was studious, coming home at five o'clock after an afternoon of athletics and schoolwork. He also had a stubborn streak. When his mother, afraid he would injure himself, told him not to play football, K.C. replied, "If I can't play, I won't go to school." By the time he was in high school, he had told his mother what he was going to do for a living: play professional basketball.

At San Francisco's Commerce High School, K.C. was a first-rate offensive player; his 18-point average was tops in the city's high school system. But one day in scrimmage, he recalls, "I made a defensive mistake, and my coach pulled me out of scrimmage and said, 'Jones, you can't play defense worth a damn.' I made up my mind to prove him wrong."

He came very close to missing his chance. There was no money for college, and he received no scholarship offers until a newsman published an interview with him describing the (fictional) offers he had received from USC, Stanford and California. The story was printed as a favor to K.C. by the writer, and it was impressive enough to get him a scholarship to the University of San Francisco. The scholarship included

$30 a month for spending money. In his sophomore year, he was assigned to room with a freshman named Bill Russell (whose scholarship provided no spending money), and he generously kept Russell from destitution through the first few months of their college careers. (According to Russell, during their first month as roommates Jones said absolutely nothing beyond what was needed to awaken Russell in the morning. Then one day, when K.C. decided he knew Russell well enough, he walked into their room and began a nonstop monologue.)

It was Phil Woolpert, the coach at San Francisco, who was the key to developing K.C. Jones's defensive instincts. Woolpert was a coach who did not preach defense; he taught it. "It wasn't that Woolpert was talking about anything new," Jones later recalled. "It was just that he made it more important than most other coaches. We would practice against a right-handed dribbler, then against a left-handed dribbler. We learned how to make an opponent concentrate on getting rid of a ball, rather than what was happening downcourt. We practiced a full-court press."

At San Francisco, Jones all but abandoned offense to concentrate on shutting down the other team. With Bill Russell at center, the Dons had a powerful offensive weapon in the "steer shot." A teammate would shoot, and Russell would guide an errant shot into the basket (this maneuver is now outlawed as offensive goal-tending). This awesome attack made it easier for Jones to think defense, and, as it turned out, it was ideal training for his role as a Celtic. A team that fielded Bill Sharman, Sam Jones and Tom Heinsohn did not need another top shooter; it needed a defensive specialist with the tenacity of K.C. Jones. And Jones's drive was so great that it literally almost killed him: during the NCAA finals in 1956, he collapsed after a game and was rushed to the hospital. It turned out that he had played the entire game with acute appendicitis.

Jones was drafted in the second round by the Celtics in 1956 (the same draft that brought Russell and Heinsohn), but had to fulfill his military obligation first. When he was discharged in the summer of 1958, he decided to try for a professional career in football, which was at the time more established and lucrative than basketball. He tried out with the Los Angeles Rams as a defensive back, and stood a good chance of making the team, especially after an exhibition game against the New York Giants in which he forced Frank Gifford into a fumble on one play and knocked aside Roosevelt Brown on another. Soon after, however, during a midweek practice, he hurt a muscle in his right leg.

A coach who had known of K.C.'s tenacity, and the ruptured appendix incident, would have assumed that Jones would not bellyache about a trivial injury. The Ram coach in question, however, was Sid Gillman, whose reputation for sensitivity and understanding ranks a shade below that of Attila. Gillman ordered Jones to suit up and take the field. Instead, Jones quit the Rams' training camp and decided to try for a position with the Celtics. Like his namesake Sam, K.C. Jones doubted he would make the team, fearing that his poor shooting would make him unfit for pro basketball. And, according to Auerbach, some of the veteran Celtics agreed. But the coach, who was to develop a particular sense of affection for a player so clearly representative of his defense-oriented philosophy, chose K.C. over veteran Gene Conley for the last spot on the team, and Jones became a Celtic for a $7,500 contract.

Like Sam, K.C. spent much of his first years on the Celtic bench—he averaged no more than half a game's playing time until his fourth season. Throughout his career, he gained almost no statistical distinction. After Cousy retired, he led the Celtics in assists for three years, but he holds no team records at all.

Yet as early as 1960, when K.C. was still averaging less

than twenty minutes a game, Auerbach explained the role that Jones was to play throughout his career. "He can take a rival team's best backcourt player and tie him up in knots," the coach said. "In all the seasons I've been in basketball, I've never before seen a player, college or pro, who could hold his hands out all the way on defense the way K.C. does and not get tired."

For nine years, the best guards of the best pretenders to Boston's title found themselves facing those hands. In the 1965 finals against the Los Angeles Lakers, K.C. won the fourth game for Boston by keeping Jerry West out of the flow of the offense until the Celtics had the game put away. Three times Boston beat the Cincinnati Royals in the playoffs during the dynasty years, and three times K.C. Jones contained Oscar Robertson.

In talking about his play, Jones once described his technique this way: "I keep my eye on his midriff and try to keep one hand touching his shirt. That usually gives me the signal when he's going to move, and which way he's going to move. In the meantime, I keep after him with my other hand, trying to slap the ball away or ruin his timing so that he has to hurry his shot or pass."

He was less complicated in describing his offense: "I had no offense," he said years later. "I tried to hide my scoring problem with my defense." In fact, however, K.C.'s offense was an important factor in perpetuating the Celtic victory string after the 1963 retirement of Bob Cousy. In that first post-Cousy season, when Bostonians were wondering whether the Celtics could win without "Mr. Basketball," K.C. Jones became the key playmaker for the team, running the fast break.

But the key to Jones's value to the Celtics lies in an observation he once made—one which Celtic after Celtic echoed, each about himself. "I don't think I could have played for any other team in the league besides the Celtics," he said. "I can't shoot, and I don't think any other club could have afforded to keep a player like me. I'm lucky in that I was allowed to concentrate almost entirely on defense. And if it wasn't this way, I don't think I could have done the job. Defense is the kind of thing you have to give your full concentration to."

In other words, as with so many other players on the Boston team, K.C. Jones was permitted to concentrate on his strength and let others compensate for his weaknesses. He was permitted, on almost every occasion, to forget about his scoring inability, and to spend his time shutting down the Jerry Wests, the Oscar Robertsons, the backcourt power of the opponents.

But there was one time of year when the perennially money-short Celtics "encouraged" Jones to meditate on his scoring inability. That was contract time. Jones even claimed, in fact, that he was so unsure about his worth that he was afraid to ask for a pay increase for fear of losing his job. "I didn't shoot well, I was only six-one. I had no wedge," he recalled. "So I just played for about the minimum salary for all those years." On another occasion, he remembered that he would "sit down for twelve hours and negotiate with Red for a two-thousand-dollar raise. When you left the table, he made you feel like you were stealing."

Apart from his defensive play, K.C. Jones achieved another, less tangible measure of worth. He became one of the best-liked Celtics ever to put on a uniform. His personality was low-key, the reverse of the effusive Heinsohn. He was also, by contrast to the often moody Russell, a far less abrasive, far more welcome black athlete. (Although he, too, was reminded of his color when his wife went looking for a place to live and was met by the sorry-it's-just-been-rented ploy. "What's the matter?" he asked his wife. "You find out we weren't white?")

In fact, K.C. Jones's career in Boston was a parallel of his first days with Bill Russell when, after a month of silence, he began to suddenly pour out the things he had been too shy to say. While playing without visible emotion on the court, he was a gifted mimic, a quietly funny humorist, and a frustrated singer who began to stop by the 99 Club regularly after a game to sing along with the pianist. When he finally left the Boston area for a West Coast coaching job, he was given a historically overcrowded party at the club.

And, in his own quiet way, K.C. Jones was doing something else in those nine years at Boston. He had spent four of those years on the bench, watching and absorbing some lessons. He had begun to develop an individualistic mix of ideas about basketball: borrowing from the Auerbach Celtics a commitment to defense and the fast break, but rejecting the idea that the way to reach players was to act as an authoritarian figure. One day, he would apply these ideas and surprise people who had regarded him as an agreeable fellow without the drive to succeed as a professional coach.

10

John Havlicek: The Unsung Hero

By the time he is finished playing basketball—assuming he is not in a Celtic uniform when America celebrates its Tricentennial—John Havlicek will have long been recognized as one of the best professional basketball players of all time. By 1976, he was making nearly a quarter of a million dollars a year; he had played in eleven straight All-Star games, starting in 1966; he was the all-time Celtic scoring leader and one of the half-dozen top scorers in NBA history; and he was approaching the record for most games played.

Yet so integrated a team was the Celtics, and so committed to the "anti-flamboyant" team style of play, that John Havlicek was not recognized as a superstar until after the dynasty years. It took the departure of Bill Russell and Sam Jones and the Celtics' slow climb back to the top to bring Havlicek recognition from the press and the public. Red Auerbach called him "the embodiment of everything the Celtics have tried to be," and the slowness of fans to recognize him was partly *because* he embodied the team's philosophy.

From the time he arrived in 1962, Havlicek fit into whatever role the Celtics designed for him—starter or sixth man, forward or guard. And he did so in a peculiarly Celtic way. For Havlicek became a superstar not with spectacular moves but with tenacity, tirelessness and unobtrusive basketball talent.

His methodical shooting, his accurate passes, his fierce but internal competitive drive were at first taken for granted. In fact, Havlicek's greatness, like Sherlock Holmes's dog that did not bark in the night, lies in what he is not. He is nothing but a pure, relentless basketball player, matching his skills and his intelligence with ceaseless energy. He has survived both good years and bad; he has, seemingly without effort or fanfare, done almost every basketball job; he has triggered the fast break, led it, trailed it, shot the baskets when the break didn't work.

One of his rivals, forward Jim McMillian, once said, "He's not very graceful, and I don't think he's very 'talented.' But every night he just seems to come out here and do the job. Look at forwards like a Spencer Haywood or a Sidney Wicks. I wouldn't consider Havlicek in that category. And you ask, 'How is he able to do this year after year?' He'll hit the jump shot, hit the lay-up, get the foul, and that's it. Very seldom does he look like he has as many points as he ends up with. And he hurts you with his passing, his defense, and the fact that he's the leader, which you can't put on a stat sheet. And I just do not understand how he can run the way he has run for all those years. He never seems to get tired. When you play against Havlicek, you get to the point where you say to yourself, 'Well, I see I'm going to have to sacrifice myself offensively, and just concentrate on stopping him.' "

Havlicek's talent for understatement is the key to much of the Celtic success. No one Celtic draws the magnetic stare of rivals and fans the moment he hits the court. No one player sparks the offense with theatrical moves and leaping shots. In a game that has always had the big-city quality of

ego around it and where the style of spectacular black athletes has become increasingly dominant, the Celtics—whatever the color of the men who played for them—played with
the style of small-town Midwesterners, subordinating in-
dividuality to the business of putting the ball in the basket.
Only the speed of the Celtic teams is testament to Red Auerbach's New York origins. The game is, in a cultural sense,
a "white" game, and John Havlicek is the exemplar of
"white" ball.

In some ways, John Havlicek's background resembles
Frank Ramsey's. He was born in a small town (Martin's
Ferry, Ohio), became a high school athletic star (baseball,
football, basketball, track, swimming), then went to the state
university (Ohio State). His college teams compiled a record
of 78–6, winning the Big Ten championship three years
straight and reaching the NCAA finals each year.

Unlike Ramsey—but like K.C. Jones and Satch Sanders—
Havlicek was not the star of his winning team. He played in
the shadow of Jerry Lucas and Larry Siegfried, and was
overshadowed as well by such Big Ten stars as Iowa's Don
Nelson and Purdue's Terry Dischinger.

Havlicek did not originally set out on a basketball career.
Although he never played college football (much to the dismay of Ohio State football coach Woody Hayes), he was
drafted by the Cleveland Browns. He tried out as a receiver
but was cut just before the 1962 season opened—no disgrace
on a team that included receivers Paul Warfield and Gary
Collins. Auerbach later said, "The biggest mistake the Cleveland Browns ever made was when they let him go, because
they were trying him for end when in my opinion he would
have been the greatest—*the greatest*—defensive back in the
history of pro football." The Browns did not have the fore-
sight, however, and Havlicek found himself in the Celtic
training camp.

Havlicek resembled Ramsey in another significant way.

In his first season with the Celtics, he seemed to fit in with the team without making the kind of mistakes expected of a rookie. In fact, Havlicek never had a typical Celtic "rookie season." Instead of sitting on the bench waiting for "garbage time," Havlicek played 2,200 minutes and averaged more than 14 points a game. Teammates were amazed by his "court presence," his willingness to take his shots even when he was missing, his lack of jitters in crucial situations. In a key playoff game against Cincinnati in 1963, he scored 23 points to give Boston a 3–2 lead. And throughout the dynasty years, he quietly became more and more important to the team. He played guard in his first three seasons, then switched to forward after Tom Heinsohn's retirement, increasing his playing time from 2,200 minutes to more than 3,000 in the Celtics' last championship season. His scoring punch—for a time he inherited Heinsohn's "gunner" reputation—made him a consistent 18- to 20-point scorer, and his offensive reputation reached a kind of peak in 1969 when, in the championship game against the Lakers, he scored 40 points. Boston won, 120–117. (His 29 points against Philadelphia in the fifth game of the semifinals had been instrumental in getting the team into the finals in the first place.)

Particularly in the last years of the dynasty, Havlicek was a largely unsung hero. In each of Russell's three seasons as coach, Havlicek was the team's leading scorer, and in the last two of those years he was the team's leading playmaker as well. In the playoffs each year, his scoring average was higher than it had been during the regular season. More important, he was able to play whatever position and role was needed on a team that had begun to lose its depth. His versatility was a stark contrast to his teammates, most of whom were specialists confined to narrower responsibilities. At least one long-time observer of the Celtics is convinced that without

Havlicek Boston would not have won a single NBA title after 1964.

Ironically, his versatility hid his value from many Boston fans. The more venerable symbols of dynasty—Russell and the Joneses—were aging, and fans began to wonder if the team could get along without one, then without another. Meanwhile, Havlicek was not so much ignored as taken for granted even though he was one of the true indispensables. Only when Russell and the Joneses retired did Havlicek begin to stand out. Only then did the press and the fans begin to reconsider his contributions to the world's greatest team.

11

Satch Sanders and Don Nelson: Help at the End of the Road

When Red Auerbach dropped the coaching reins of the Celtics to center Bill Russell after the 1966 season, the dynasty was already on its last legs. They lost in the championship in 1967 to the towering Philadelphia 76ers. And although they recaptured the title in the 1968 and 1969 *playoffs,* their regular-season finishes—second and fourth—were more accurate reflections of their diminishing strength.

Sam Jones and Bill Russell still anchored the team, and John Havlicek's consistency and versatility were crucial. But the Celtics had to win without the depth of past years, and to do so, they collected players who lacked superstar talent, but who made critical contributions all the same. Bailey Howell, obtained from the Bullets for Mel Counts in one of the few player trades in Celtic history, became a high-scoring power forward (19–20 points per game in each of his first three seasons) who played a key role in the Celtic victory over Los Angeles in the 1968 playoff finals. Larry Siegfried gave Boston seven seasons of consistent backcourt shooting power. Wayne Embry, a six-eight enforcer who came over from Cincinnati in 1966, gave the Celtics off-the-bench muscle under the boards the year they reclaimed the title in 1968.

But if there were two players who characterized the capacity of the Celtics to get consistently valuable play out of men without superstar capacity, they would be Tom "Satch" Sanders and Don Nelson. Both men arrived without any confidence that they would fit in with the Boston Celtics. Yet each wound up giving more than a decade. Both absorbed the essential spirit of Celtic play, and helped teach it to the next generation of Celtics. Both combined moderate ability with sharp intelligence, and made that intelligence compensate for the purely physical skills they lacked.

•

Tom "Satch" Sanders grew up in Harlem, on Lenox Avenue at 116th Street, in a neighborhood poor in wealth and in spirit. He was gifted, both athletically and intellectually. His mother recalls that "he was always a much better reader than most of the kids in the neighborhood, and they would sit around and he would read to them or tell them stories from the books."

He went to Seward Park High School, where his first love was baseball. It was his appearance on the pitcher's mound, in fact, that won him his nickname; to some observers, he resembled the ageless Satchel Paige. But two bridges stood between Sanders and a baseball career: his upper bridge and his lower bridge.

"I didn't stay a pitcher long, because I treasured my teeth," Sanders recalls. "I developed a bad habit of catching the ball with my mouth, and it got to be a painful experience every time I went to the mound." Dreading the day when his curveball didn't break—and fearing the day when his jawbone did—Sanders finally decided "it was time to take up another game." In Harlem, that game was basketball.

The six-six Sanders played the pivot position at Seward Park, and developed some impressive back-to-the-basket moves. In sharp contrast to the typical playground player, however, Sanders found another source of satisfaction to the game: defense. "I quickly discovered," he said, "that there was no thrill to shooting. I felt that if I shot I was leaving the other kids out of the game."

Sanders won a scholarship to New York University. Like several other Celtics, he played for a time in the shadow of a more prominent player, All-American Cal Ramsey. Ramsey remembers Sanders' lack of coordination as a teenager and his determination to improve: "When we were both at NYU, he lifted weights to toughen himself for the college game. He started walking erect to make the most of his height to the point where we called him 'Mr. Posture.' "

In Sanders' senior year, after Ramsey had left NYU to try a career in the pros, Sanders came into his own. He broke eight Violet records, and captained the team to a 22–5 record. But the presence elsewhere of collegiate stars—Oscar Robertson, Jerry Lucas and Jerry West, to name three—kept him off the All-America list, and off the 1960 Olympic team. The Celtics, who as usual had the last draft choice, picked Sanders in the first round, largely on the insistence of NYU coach Lou Rossini that Sanders was an exceptional defensive player. Sanders had a job offer from the Tuck Tape Company, and almost didn't show up for the Celtic tryout. And Auerbach was horrified by the player who did appear. Sanders played with knee guards and glasses, which slowed his game considerably. So Auerbach and his players adopted a handy expedient: they hid his excess equipment, and Sanders soon proved to be a swift, effective player.

The presence of Sanders in the Celtic front line was so fortuitous that Auerbach might have built him had he not existed. In 1960, Auerbach had the most intimidating defensive center the game had seen. In K.C. Jones, he was developing the most effective defensive backcourt man. Now, with Sanders, Auerbach had the only missing piece: a corner man who could shut down the scoring threat in the front line. The agressive play he brought to this task is reflected in the only statistical category in which Sanders ever led his team: for five straight years, he accumulated more personal fouls than anyone else on the Celtics, and was constantly among NBA leaders in fouling out. But he was no "hatchet man"; rather, he was doing the job he was paid to do: intimidating the opposition's high scoring forwards, and helping to force the ball out of the corners and into the middle, where Russell was waiting.

When Chet Walker played for Philadelphia, he described Sanders' ability this way: "He's the best, no question about it. A lot of guys are down at that end of the court just killing time. But defense is bread and butter to Satch, and he never forgets it for a second. I have a real hard time getting free from him to get the ball. One reason is because he plays me with his hands. His hands are always on me, feeling so he knows where I am. At the same time, his eyes are on the ball."

It was this formula that enabled Sanders to shut down the opposition at critical times in the Celtics' playoff history, such as the 1966 seventh game in Los Angeles, when he held Elgin Baylor to 2 points in the first half.

As with so many of his teammates, Sanders never permitted himself to believe that his skills earned him the right to any security. Playing defense, forgoing the scoring statistics, Sanders looked at every training camp as a new threat to his job security. "There are seniors graduating from college every year that want to play pro ball," he said midway through his career. "It's kind of brutal, cruel, because you come face to face with the fellow . . . This is the law of the jungle."

And Sanders followed another Celtic tradition. Many of

the Boston players who were not outstanding stars of the game found themselves honored by Boston fans for longevity, for assuming the role of elder. K.C. Jones and John Havlicek both grew in stature as they returned year after year. So, too, did Sanders. His last years with Boston were far from his most productive. From 1969 to 1971, he was slowed by injuries, and in his last two years he was a substitute who was used less and less frequently. But on the Celtic bench, swathed in towels like a wise man of the Orient, he became a comforting figure to the Celtic crowds, and his rare appearances on the court drew cheers of approval. Sanders, in sum, had become to the fans a part of the team's history and tradition.

He had also become convinced that his career could not be confined to athletics. He was one of the founders of Athletes for a Better Urban Society, and as a businessman won a federal grant to rehabilitate housing in Boston's inner-city neighborhoods of Roxbury and South Dorchester. And he was, by the end of his career, seeking to drive home the lesson that the path to success he traveled was a very narrow one.

"Every kid wants to be a professional basketball player," he said in 1975. "Okay, don't try to tell him that he can't make it. But try to get across to him the idea that he should be prepared for something else. Set up a list of priorities. All right, so basketball is number one. But what's next? Don't get stuck in a situation where you have to face the grim reality that you have no future in basketball and have nothing else to fall back on. Believe me, I saw that happen to some of my teammates on the Celtics. And it wasn't a very happy thing to see."

Yet this sharp sense of the limits of basketball did nothing to lessen the sense of satisfaction that Sanders drew from the way the Celtics dominated their sport. At the press conference announcing his appointment as Harvard's head basketball coach, Sanders made a statement that might be dis-

missed as corn were it not for the consistency of the sentiment among Celtics. "I'll go on preaching the Celtics' life,"
he said. "I happen to feel this is the way things ought to be
in sports, and in everything else we do."

•

If Tom Sanders held doubts about his place on the Celtics
throughout his career, he was the victim of terminal over-
confidence compared to Don Nelson. Frequently, Red Auerbach would find an unwanted player and get additional value
out of him. Gene Conley came back when his pitching career
ended. Willie Naulls, Em Bryant, Carl Braun all gave service
after their careers seemed over. But Nelson didn't even have
much achievement behind him.

No one ever came into the Boston Garden with more
uncertainty about his future than Nelson. And, whether out
of determination or desperation, no one more thoroughly
demonstrated the Celtic habit of picking a player for a limited set of skills. He spent more than a decade with the team
and, with Havlicek, was the last active player linked to the
dynasty. And by doing what he did well, he earned for
himself an important place on the roster of Bostonians who
have helped to perpetuate and revive the unique spirit of the
Celtics.

Don Nelson was born in 1940 in Muskegon, Michigan, and
raised on a farm outside Rock Island, Illinois. His family had
little money, and the conditions under which he developed
his basketball skills were adverse in the strictest sense of that
word. "My dad had rigged up a basket in the yard which was
just covered with chicken shit," he remembers. "If I missed
a shot, the ball would roll all over the place and get filthy."
It was a harsh way to learn accuracy, and at Rock Island
High School he learned another harsh lesson about the com-

petitive spirit. "Our coach thought we were dogging it," he
says, "and one day he just locked us in the gym and had us
beat the hell out of each other. I don't know if that was it,
but I think we started to win more games after that."

Nelson won a scholarship to the University of Iowa. As a
six-six center, he broke every school scoring record and was
twice named to the All-Conference team. But when his professional career got under way, it looked as if his dream of
success was going to turn sour. After a year with the Chicago
Zephyrs, who were sinking quickly into the Midwestern
swamp, Nelson went to the Los Angeles Lakers. In his second year there, he spent virtually the entire season on the
bench. Then, three days into the 1965–66 season, he was
placed on waivers. He went home to Moline, Illinois . . . and
waited for the telephone to ring.

"There was no place to go," he recalls. "Nobody even
contacted me from the Eastern League. I didn't want to call
the Lakers, because I was too embarassed. So I just sat
around. The fifth day, I got a call from Auerbach, and he
asked me if I wanted to try out with the Celtics. I told him
I'd die, I'd do anything for a tryout."

He remembers listening to a Celtic game from St. Louis,
taking heart from a Celtic loss in which Ron Watts, the man
he had to beat out for a job, did not do well. (Watts did a
lot better years later as Bill Russell's friend in a now-famous
commercial.) He remembers traveling to Boston, staying at
the Lenox Hotel—the same hotel in which Auerbach lived
—and sweating out the time until the Celtics came home; he
was too timid to call the team offices to find out where he
could work out. "I look back on it and realize how dumb it
was," he says, "because I was out of shape, terribly out of
shape. It was about the worst thing I could have done."

When Nelson finally got his chance to fight for a job with
Boston, putting his career on the line in a two- or three-day
stretch of scrimmages, what did he do? "I can't remember

a thing about what I did except getting so exhausted I almost threw up."

His teammate Bill Russell, however, remembers Nelson demonstrating a skilled shooting eye against three Celtic forwards. And Tom Heinsohn, who had recently retired but who attended these Celtic workouts, recalls, "I was very high on him. He was very deceiving. You couldn't get around him on offense because he was very cute. He knew exactly how to play you, and he had a clever way of hooking you."

After the workout, Watts was cut from the team and Nelson had a job. A decade later, he still had it.

In the last three years of the Russell era, Nelson steadily gained playing time, from 1,202 minutes in 1967 to 1,773 in 1968–69. Playing a little less than half the time, he averaged 11.6 points a game in Russell's last year, and his shooting percentage was near .500.

Nelson's full value would not be realized until after the collapse and resurrection of the team, but his presence throughout the last years of the Boston Celtic record could have served as a symbol of what Auerbach had created. For it was not simply with the publicized, extraordinarily gifted stars that Auerbach won so often; it was also with a group of second-platoon players who were used brilliantly at their often restricted specialties. The team was still able to win titles when on paper the talent simply wasn't there.

Part Three
Aftermath

12

The Team

In 1972, Red Auerbach stood up to address the Chamber of Commerce Executive Club in Boston. He began his remarks with characteristic bluntness:

"Let me start by saying that this is not quite the honor, my being here, that you think it is. I haven't had too much respect for the Chamber of Commerce over my years in Boston. When the Celtics won eleven championships in thirteen years, and were practically ignored in their own town, then how could I feel otherwise?"

Auerbach's accusation was harsh but true. And not only did the Celtics lack public support. One of the most astonishing facts about the Boston Celtics was that throughout their existence—from the early years through the dynasty season and all the way to the present—they were without any sense of financial security. While the team built an unparalleled record of success, and while those who had formed the nucleus of the dynasty went on to success in off-the-court activities, the franchise itself was surrounded by never-ending front-office turmoil. And when the dynasty abruptly ended in 1969 with the retirement of Bill Russell, the team seemed to face failure from the pivot to the balance sheets.

The Celtics were a "poor" club throughout the years of Walter Brown's and Lou Pieri's ownership—one year's worth of travel was charged to Pieri's credit card because airlines and hotels would not accept the Celtics' credit. But the commitment of these men provided a sense of stability anyway. Financial hardship forced some incredible economies on the team. Tom Heinsohn recalls, "It got so bad in some years that they used to close down the offices right after our last playoff game. So there was no publicity, nothing during the off-season. That had to hurt us, but I guess they couldn't afford to keep them open all summer."

The Garden itself owned the Boston Bruins, and despite Walter Brown's influence, the Bruins always came first in terms of playing dates. (Bob Schmertz, who owned the team in the 1970's, claimed the Garden charged the Celtics enough rent to pay the entire year-round expenses of the arena.) Still, Brown's dedication to the team and his willingness to underwrite its losses provided some security in the early dynasty years.

But the pressure—of finances, and of Brown's own compulsive work habits—finally brought him down. On Labor Day in 1964, as workmen frantically labored to put the finishing touches on his new offices in the Garden, Walter Brown suffered a fatal heart attack on Cape Cod during one of his rare vacations. At his death, his estate was valued at $430,000—substantially less than it might have been—plus the team whose market value he had helped secure. The following year, the team was sold to entrepreneur Marvin Kratter for $2.6 million. And Red Auerbach, who had been given 10 percent of the Celtic stock as a reward for his years of service, made $300,000 on the sale of his stock to Kratter.

Kratter's company was not satisfied, however. After a few

years, they realized that with the enormous expenses of rent
to the Garden, escalating salary costs and indifferent attendance, the Celtics were bringing in $880,000 a year and costing
$850,000—a profit of $30,000 on an investment of $3 million,
a return much poorer (and less certain) than U.S. Savings
Bonds, and not that much better than keeping the money in
a mattress. The Board of Directors compelled Kratter to sell
the Celtics in 1968 to Ballantine Breweries, which in turn sold
the club in 1970 to a conglomerate called Trans National
Communications, headed by E. Ellis Erdman. Bob Ryan of
the Boston *Globe* has described what happened next in his
book *Celtic Pride:*

"One after another of [TNC's] holdings ran into trouble.
Things got so bad that the Celtics soon became their only
source of income. If the team played on a Wednesday night,
a TNC man was up from New York on Thursday to grab the
gate receipts . . .

"[In the 70–71 season] pay checks began to bounce. The
team fell seriously behind in its bill paying, eventually owing
upwards of sixty thousand dollars to American Airlines.
Hotels around the league barred the team, some for years
afterward. Worst of all, Travelers' Insurance Company
cancelled the Celtics' team accident insurance policy because TNC couldn't come up with the annual premium of
$7,424.69."

Rumors began to spread that TNC was in trouble. Erdman denied them with a flourish, revealing plans for building
a new arena to be ready for the 1973 season. It was to seat
12,500 fans, hardly an optimistic projection of the Celtics'
drawing power. But when TNC failed to make payments on
its purchase of the team, Ballantine sued and got it back. A
year later, in 1972, the team was sold for $5 million to Bob
Schmertz, a millionaire promoter of "leisure technology"
and owner of the New England Whalers.

With Schmertz in power, things seemed secure. But the

Celtic luck remained unhappily consistent. The "leisure technology" market collapsed in the wake of the 1974 recession and energy crisis, eradicating Schmertz's financial base. That same year, Schmertz was indicted by a grand jury for attempting to bribe land officials in New Jersey. In the summer of 1975, the forty-eight-year-old Schmertz died of a stroke in New York. (The team is now controlled by Irving Levin and Harold Lipton, two West Coast businessmen.)

Ironically, the management follies of the Celtics continued even when the team began to attract new paying customers. In 1970, the team's worst year, attendance was up. And by 1974–75 the Celtics were actually outdrawing the invincible Bruin hockey team. There were many possible explanations:

•The Celtic fans got more interested having tasted defeat.

•The massive college population of Boston, many from the New York area, was hooked on basketball and came to Celtic games to watch good pro ball without having to mortgage their souls for tickets.

•Network television brought a more sophisticated appreciation of talent to all fans, Boston's included.

And the Celtics were without the controversial, outspoken Bill Russell. The heart and soul of the team were John Havlicek and Dave Cowens, the center who battled for rebounds as if plenary indulgences were contained inside each basketball. Cowens was Catholic and red-headed. His ancestry was not Irish, but the Celtic management did not go out of its way to so inform the fans. There was, to be blunt about it, a core of talented white players with whom the fans could identify, as well as the black stars like Paul Silas and Jo Jo White.

While owners came and went with regularity, and fans began to show up consistently, the team collapsed, then began to rebuild. This five-year-long drama demonstrated that Auerbach's philosophy, which had come to be taken for granted during the dynasty years, had enduring value. Throughout the thirteen years of Celtic domination, many of

Auerbach's critics had deprecated his role, pointing out the team's remarkable talent and choosing to forget that Auerbach had, often with unparalleled shrewdness, put this talent together. When Auerbach retired as coach, he still retained the key to victory by appointing as his successor Bill Russell, whose coaching was aided by the on-court presence of center Bill Russell.

In the summer of 1969, however, Russell announced his retirement in the pages of *Sports Illustrated,* and general manager Auerbach was faced with the job of finding a new coach at a late date (difficult) and a replacement for center Russell (impossible). Even in the 1968–69 season, the advancing age of Russell and Sam Jones had slowed the mighty Bostonians to a fourth-place regular-season finish. Now, with the last link to the early championships gone, the Celtics were without the experience, poise and personnel to continue the record of success.

For Tom Heinsohn, the hastily selected new coach, the 1969–70 season was to be a trial by ordeal. Only Havlicek and and an injury-ridden Sanders had roots far back into the winning tradition. Jo Jo White was a raw rookie; Paul Silas was playing for the Phoenix Suns; Dave Cowens was a senior at Florida State University. For the first time since Auerbach arrived, the team finished under .500. The fall was entirely predictable, but together with the wobbly financial status of the Celtics it made 1970 the low-water mark of the franchise.

If there was any consolation for Auerbach in these years of on- and off-the-court turnovers, it was the extension of Celtic success by former players—those who had begun the dynasty. Of all the teams in professional sports history, the Celtics produced the most successful coaches. At latest count, more than thirty one-time Celtics have coached at the college level. Not all have been completely successful. But all of them seem to have taken a large dose of the Celtic philosophy with them.

Some of the men who went into coaching found the outlook of their playing days essentially unchanged; more of them found that the changes in the world had forced them into taking a hard look at the premises by which they had played, and by which they had lived. But all of them seemed to employ a central Auerbach thesis: that what a coach could bring to the team he led was less a sense of strategy, and more a sense of excellence.

13

The Drive for Success

The will to win, of which so much is made in sports autobiographies, is bound up with the desire for success—both for the recognition and for the material rewards that victory can bring. The night of the seventh game of the 1957 NBA finals, Red Auerbach's locker room speech was aimed squarely at his players' goals. "Defense and dollars," he said, "dollars and defense." To a child of poverty or of just-scraping-by status who is also gifted with exceptional athletic skill, the will to win is especially tied to the desire for big money and fame.

For some athletes, financial security is enough. Once they can buy the space and serenity denied them in their childhood (many have bought farmland—the breathing room they lacked as children), they relax. For others, however, success does not curb the competitive drive. Instead, it burns on, like a flame independent of fuel. So many seasons, so many games, from childhood through maturity, have triggered that drive that these athletes cannot shake the feeling that all life is competition, and that all enterprises are do-or-die tests.

•

Bob Cousy, Frank Ramsey, and Bill Sharman were three of the Celtic heroes who could turn their abilities to maximum effectiveness on the basketball court. Each of them was financially successful once his playing career was over. But there the similarity ends. For Bob Cousy, staying in the game led to emotional agony, and to doubts that the passion for victory was really the unmitigated good he once thought it to be. For Frank Ramsey, success in business replaced the world of sports, and basketball became a sideline. But for Bill Sharman, the dogged, methodical determination to win persisted, until personal tragedy invaded his carefully ordered world.

When Bob Cousy left the Celtics for the coaching position at Boston College in 1963, he took with him a determination to win that had already affected him emotionally and physically. Now he sat on the Boston College bench again without the exorcism of physical competition. He recalls a trip up to Dartmouth early in his coaching career, when he thought he was about to die: "I remember being on a couch and having to crawl across the room. The pain was so bad I couldn't walk to the game. Later, while we were in the hotel lobby, the players kept bringing their parents over to meet Bob Cousy, and I was sitting completely crouched over; I couldn't stand up to meet them." When he went to the hospital, expecting to find he was suffering a heart attack or a perforated ulcer, he discovered instead it was gas: an attack so severe it had, he was told, literally twisted his guts.

Throughout his six years as Boston College coach—six successful years with winning records and invitations to the NIT and NCAA tournaments—the pains stayed with him:

severe chest pains, stomach pains, outbreaks of cold sweat. Winning, he began to realize, did not lessen the tension; winning *intensified* it. And there were other pressures as well.

In 1967, a *Life* magazine story linked Cousy to a couple of Springfield gamblers, one of whom Cousy acknowledged as a close friend. Nothing illegal or unethical was ever established, but for the first time in his career Cousy found himself attacked by the Boston press which had deified him for so long.

"People who seek out public support and approbation have an obligation to be, like Caesar's wife, above suspicion," a Boston *Globe* editorial argued. "Cousy, by his own choice, has not fulfilled this obligation nearly as well as he might have."

Friendship with a gambler was a rare crack in Cousy's good-guy image—it is hard to remember how athletes were then looked up to. He resented what he considered unfair accusations but managed to ride out the bad publicity.

The conditions of college coaching, however, presented him with a more fundamental problem. Cousy was Auerbach's first choice to coach the Celtics after he left the bench in 1966, but he turned down the job because, he said, "I had signed a contract at Boston College, and I also didn't want to coach the players I played with." But he found that the college level had its own special pressures. Specifically, the demand for top high school basketball talent was so great that big-time colleges recruited with far more than the rulebook allowed: gut courses, ready cash, girls, in one case a woman for the *father* of a player.

Cousy had built Boston College into a winning team, reaching the NIT finals in 1969. But the unfairly competitive recruiting situation and contradictions of imposing discipline on athletes who had been begged to come to the school made the pressures too great. Finally, when the son of a long-time family friend was not permitted to attend BC because he had once attended Cousy's basketball camp—a technical violation of the recruiting rules that were bent or broken a hundred times a year at other institutions—Cousy handed in his resignation. He promptly took on an even more pressure-filled situation.

He had long maintained that professional coaching was simply too intense an experience for him to try—an opinion shared by Auerbach, who pointed to Cousy's emotional state during the far shorter college season. But in 1969 the Cincinnati Royals made him an offer he couldn't refuse: a three-year, half-a-million-dollar contract to make a winner—and a fan attraction—out of the Cincinnati Royals.

From the financial point of view—gaining radio and television contracts and ultimately increasing the value of the franchise—Cousy's tenure was successful. But from the point of view that had been the Celtics' only guiding principle—winning—Cousy's years were marked by failure. For perhaps the first time in his life, he was not part of a winning operation. In the course of four and a half years, his teams won 141 games and lost 207. Cousy failed to establish a working relationship with Oscar Robertson, traded away the gifted but lackadaisical Jerry Lucas, then, desperate for a back-up center, traded away young Norm Van Lier. That trade sparked rumors that Cousy wanted to separate Van Lier and Cousy's daughter, who had been dating. More serious for the team, Cousy got no useful players in the trades and had only moderate success in the drafts.

Only in the acquisition and use of Nate "Tiny" Archibald did Cousy demonstrate a tangible achievement. The 1970 draft choice from Texas–El Paso was a player in the Cousy mold: a dazzling playmaker and shooter, whose court sense was astonishing. In 1972, realizing that the Kansas City Kings (just arrived from Cincinnati) had no chance of making the playoffs, Cousy decided to make Archibald the center of attention, and told him to score as many points as he could. Archibald wound up leading the NBA in scoring *and* assists—the first time in the league's history that it had been done. Archibald's achievement paid off: attendance took the biggest one-year jump in the history of the franchise. Yet it was the kind of coaching decision that was based on the hopelessness of building a winning team, and it was the kind of decision that a Red Auerbach could hardly have imagined.

But Cousy was not Auerbach; indeed, Cousy was not the same Cousy that had spent pre-playoff afternoons working up hatreds against the man he would be guarding. The dissenter in Cousy, the part that persuaded him to help organize the Players' Association, was causing him to doubt the country's direction and his own. In 1972, for example, he campaigned for Republican peace candidate Pete McCloskey in the New Hampshire primary. And when the Watergate affair threw the "winning is everything" philosophy into sharper doubt, Cousy began to question whether the competitive philosophy by which he had lived was really that valuable. He wrote a book, *Killer Instinct,* in which he attacked "a grotesque over-emphasis on winning . . . a value system gone astray."

Still, this is *not* a case of a sudden conversion. It is rather part of a conflict that Cousy has lived with throughout his adult life. He has hardly turned his back on material rewards, for example. Since his resignation as Kings' coach in the middle of the 1973–74 season, Cousy has kept compulsively and profitably busy. He is Commissioner of the American Soccer League, representative for a sporting goods manufacturer, color commentator on Celtics' and New England collegiate games, all of which brings him a six-figure income. He is constantly on the move, logging more than 100,000 miles of travel a year.

And although he found today's highly paid athletes hard to coach, he harbors no personal resentment. Talking on the enclosed patio of a spectacular home in Worcester, with a powder-blue Cadillac parked outside, he said, "When I reject the notion that I was 'born ten years too soon'—before the big money in pro ball—I reject it from *these* surroundings. I signed as the number one draft choice for nine thousand dollars in 1950. David Thompson signed for what? Two million? But if I had two million dollars, my life style wouldn't change."

And as for losing? It seems less ugly now than it did during the long seasons in Cincinnati and Kansas City: "Losing *produced* my present thinking. In retrospect, it was very beneficial to me as a person. Looking back, it helped me. If you're winning all the time, you never reach that objectivity."

And yet Cousy recognizes that the drive to win has by no means been exorcised. "I'm not sure I could carry out what I say if I went back into coaching. The killer instinct is what got Boston College into the NIT finals; it's what got the Celtics all those titles. So as much as I enjoy coaching, teaching kids, I think going back to coaching would put me in an early grave."

Bob Cousy represents a halfway figure between athletes who left sports behind and those who continued to pursue it all their lives. To look, in contrast, at Frank Ramsey and at Bill Sharman is to see two Celtic heroes who are at polar opposites.

•

Frank Ramsey retired as a player in 1964, with all his skills intact, because of a happy accident. With a Kentucky friend, he had begun to build houses, and had been struck by the profitability of the construction business. Before he left the Celtics, he was already on his way to affluence as a builder.

He went home to Madisonville after retiring and became, in all probability, the wealthiest of all those who have played with the Celtics. He is a prominent businessman, director of two banks, nursing home owner, a man to be reckoned with. And he refused to be drawn into the basketball arena, except for occasional work as a color commentator for Southern Conference basketball games. In 1966, Auerbach offered Ramsey the Celtic coaching job after Cousy refused it, and Ramsey turned the offer down flat.

But in November of 1970 the Kentucky Colonels of the American Basketball Association prevailed on Ramsey to take over the coaching job in an emergency. From November until the season ended, he commuted 150 miles between Madisonville and Louisville, and led the Colonels into the ABA finals against the Utah Stars—whose coach was fellow ex-Celtic Bill Sharman. The underdog Colonels took the series to seven games, but lost.

Yet Ramsey was not attracted to the life he had given up when he left the Celtics. The distance from his home and family, and the demands of his business enterprises, were too great. So he left the coaching job after the 1970–71 season to return to Madisonville. He still maintains his friendships with the Celtics, but he—unlike almost every one of his teammates—found other pursuits and put the excitement and the spotlight of big-time basketball behind him.

•

There could be no greater contrast to the exit of Frank Ramsey than the odyssey of Bill Sharman. Despite the methodical nature of his life—mapping out hours, days and weeks, breaking each task down into its parts until each piece fell into place—Sharman moved from place to place, always searching for something better, looking for the ideal place to apply his talent and drive.

While still in college, he had left Southern California for a baseball career; hung for several years between professional baseball and professional basketball; decided to give up basketball and then at the last minute changed his mind and began his brilliant Celtic career. But the end of his playing days with Boston was the beginning of a new life with the same characteristics. Finally, back home in Southern California, he achieved his finest hour—and then watched helplessly as things fell apart, broken by events that no amount of planning, no amount of movement, could stop.

When Sharman left Boston in 1961, he signed on with the Los Angeles Jets of the newly founded American Basketball League. The Jets folded midway through the season, and Sharman was named coach of the Cleveland Pipers. The team won the ABL's first—and last—championship. When the league folded, Sharman moved on: to Cal State in Los Angeles as basketball coach, to St. Louis for a broadcasting job, and then to the San Francisco Warriors as coach. His team won the Western Division title in 1967, but Sharman's total obsession with winning was too much for the players and even for the owner.

One player called Sharman "the meanest, narrowest, most miserable son of a bitch who ever lived." And the much-traveled Rick Barry found the system intolerable. "He's a fine person," Barry told sportswriter Bill Libby. "But he's a miserable person to play under. He's fanatical about basketball. He eats, sleeps, and drinks the game . . . he's the narrowest individual I've ever known. We weren't allowed to talk about anything but basketball. We were not supposed to read anything but our basketball box scores. We were not supposed to have wives or girl friends or children or friends or homes. You weren't supposed to have good meals or parties or feelings about the world. There was no world beyond the basketball court. He just went too far, that's all."

Nate Thurmond added, "The year was hell." And Warrior

owner Franklin Mieuli offered the unusual complaint that
his coach simply cared too much about the game. "I'd walk
in in the morning and Sharman would be waiting outside my
door," Mieuli said. "All day he'd be coming into my office.
At night, when I'd try to leave, he'd be hanging on my
coattails dragging me back. He was always figuring angles.
He always had something he wanted me to do, which he
figured would help him win. I wanted a winner, and he sure
turned out to be a winner. I wanted a full-time coach, and
he turned out to be a twenty-four-hour-a-day coach. I just
got more than I bargained for. You couldn't find a sweeter
man away from the court, but he was a hard man on the
court . . . Sharman was obsessed. I didn't enjoy working with
Sharman, but I enjoyed winning with Sharman."

Sharman, who says he and Barry are now friendly, admitted to writer Libby, "I *am* very intense about basketball
. . . I was brought up one way and I'm bent one way and I
think it's the best way, which is to give the game everything
you have . . .

"I work [players] hard and make great demands on them.
In this respect, I don't think I'm much different from a Red
Auerbach or a Vince Lombardi or a George Allen or a
Walter Alston . . . The most remarkable thing about the old
Celtic teams was that as much as they won, they always
wanted to win more. They were hungrier than the teams that
should have been hungrier. They were always more willing
to risk their lives for the loose ball."

He stressed details, he said, because details can make the
difference between winning and losing. He had studied the
game and found that 40 percent of games were decided by
one point, by one basket, or in overtime. And he noted that
games, key games, championship games, were often decided
by one loose ball, one steal, one rebound. "I want my players,
I want my team, to be prepared to make the one play that
will make the difference between their winning and losing."

In 1969, Sharman left the Warriors to return once again to Los Angeles—as coach of the Los Angeles Stars of the fledgling American Basketball Association. The club owners promised him a share of the club's ownership and a pension plan generous enough to compensate him for the losses he would take in leaving the NBA.

He didn't have a strong team or enough height, but somehow he brought the Stars to the ABA playoffs. With the team's best player (Merv Jackson) and key rebounder (Zelmo Beatty) out with injuries or legal problems, the Stars beat the favored Denver Rockets for the Western title and entered the ABA finals, where they lost to the Indiana Pacers. Sharman still regards this feat as his finest coaching job of his career.

In 1970, the Stars were sold to Bill Daniels, who moved the club to Salt Lake City. Sharman took his team to the playoffs again and beat the Kentucky Colonels (coached by Frank Ramsey) in seven games to win the ABA championship.

Sharman did not even stay around for the victory party. By June of 1971, he was in Los Angeles again—as the new coach of the Los Angeles Lakers. "I want to come back to Southern California because that's my home," he said. "There is no animosity. It was a fairy tale year. It's not a matter of money; I've had offers of more money from clubs in both leagues." The Stars responded with a lawsuit to prevent his departure, which failed to keep him in Utah. The damage claim was postponed.

In taking the Laker coaching job, Sharman was approaching the most difficult task of his career. Every other team he had gone to had been floundering, thus giving the ex-Celtic a blank piece of paper to write on, a chance to build a team up from nothing. The Lakers were something else again. They had been the first great team in the National Basketball Association in the days when the bespectacled, six-ten George Mikan controlled the backboards of the league. Since moving to Los Angeles in 1960, they had never been out of the playoffs, and since 1968 they had been fielding three of the great basketball players of the age: Elgin Baylor, Jerry West and Wilt Chamberlain. But never had they brought a title to Los Angeles, and now their stars were getting old.

"When I took this job," Sharman told me, "everybody said I was kind of crazy, because the Lakers had Baylor, Wilt, Jerry, and they were all old. Baylor was about thirty-seven, West was thirty-three, Wilt was thirty-five, and everybody said, 'That team's too old, you can't win, so you'll have to start all over again.' "

He hired ex-Celtic K.C. Jones as assistant coach and resident expert on defense. But Sharman's first job was to establish a relationship with Wilt Chamberlain, whose stormy relationships with past coaches had earned him the reputation of being uncoachable. Chamberlain respected Sharman, but Sharman wanted to be sure of coaxing—rather than attempting to bludgeon—Chamberlain into playing the kind of fast-break-oriented basketball Sharman had learned at Boston.

"I invited Wilt out to lunch," he recalls, "because I wanted to sound him out about the way he felt he should play and how the team should be structured, and how we could put the whole thing together. We went over a lot of things— should he play high post or low post, should we fast-break, should he shoot more or not. I was very impressed because he mentioned a lot of things that wouldn't necessarily help his career, but would help the Lakers. He felt with the shooters we had, he didn't need to score as much, that he'd rather set picks and pass off more. And he felt the running game, which didn't necessarily help him at the age of thirty-five, would help the team to fast-break more.

"But the thing I *really* remember about that lunch," Sharman adds with a smile, "is that I left my wallet at home and if the owner hadn't recognized us and picked up the check,

I would have had to borrow money from Chamberlain."

Wilt was impressed enough to agree to Sharman's regimen, including the daily 11 A.M. practice sessions that for a night-life-loving insomniac like Chamberlain were a special agony.

And, according to long-time Laker announcer (and assistant general manager) Chick Hearn, the Sharman method convinced the other Lakers as well: "Sharman was—is—the most dedicated man I've ever seen. We would play a game, let's say at the Boston Garden, and he'd come out while the other guys were reading the stat sheets on the game, he'd be sitting in his seat with the bus light on, working on tomorrow night's plays in Chicago. He is just totally, *totally* involved. I've never seen a coach so involved. I've seen other coaches, particularly when you win, go out and have a beer, they're having fun. Not Bill. Totally involved, getting ready for the next game."

During that 1971–72 season, it all seemed to come together. A thirty-three-game winning streak (an all-time record), the championship, the Coach of the Year award for Sharman. And then it all began to unravel.

Start with the least painful of Sharman's burdens, the loss of his voice. Shortly after the 1972 seasons, his voice disappeared. Sharman was not a demonstrative coach in the Tommy Heinsohn sense, but he was a shouter, an instructor, barking out warnings and advice to his teammates in noisy, crowded arenas for more than a decade. He had never learned to speak correctly, using his throat muscles rather than his diaphragm. After the end of the 1972 season, he spent the better part of two years unable to speak above a whisper, scribbling out his instructions to his players and assistants on pieces of paper.

In 1973, the Lakers once again reached the finals of the NBA, but a Knick team, getting one last performance out of the crippled Willis Reed, beat them in five games, taking the last four in a row. And after the 1973 playoffs, Chamberlain, still an imposing defensive player and rebounder despite his thirty-seven years, quit the Lakers to become player-coach of the San Diego Conquistadors. In 1974, Los Angeles stumbled into the playoffs thanks to an injury to Nate Thurmond of the Warriors. But they got whipped by Milwaukee in five games.

At the start of 1974, Los Angeles was hit again; just before the season opened, Laker stalwart Jerry West retired. That opened the floodgates of bad luck for the team. Injuries decimated Sharman's team; by the end of the season, no Laker would have missed fewer than eight games. Thus, Los Angeles played its season with new personnel, hastily assembled after the season had started, and with predictable results. The once-mighty Lakers finished the 1974–75 season with the second worst record in the NBA. Only the first-year New Orleans Jazz lost more games.

It is a measure of Sharman's misfortunes that the collapse of his team and the loss of his voice became trivial, almost insignificant events.

After twenty years of marriage to Ileana Bough, Sharman was divorced in 1968 and a few months later married his second wife, Dorothy. An athletic woman, she fit perfectly into Sharman's new life style in California. The two had a home in Palos Verdes built right on a country club, and they played golf or tennis every day. Then, in the fall of 1972, Dorothy began complaining of back pains. At first, doctors could find nothing wrong. When they finally did, it was too late. Dorothy had cancer. There were long sessions at the Sloan-Kettering Cancer Center in New York, cross-country flights by Sharman to visit his ailing wife, and an endless series of operations which weakened Dorothy, but could do nothing to help. In early 1974, she died.

Dorothy's daughter by an earlier marriage had lived with

the Sharmans, but after her mother's death she moved back with her father. Sharman was alone; he closed the house and moved into an apartment at Marina del Rey. And a few weeks after his wife died, heading for an airplane in the Houston airport, Sharman heard himself summoned to a white courtesy phone. The voice on the other end told him his seventy-seven-year-old father had died suddenly of a heart attack. And shortly after that, Sharman was assessed a $250,000 damage finding in a breach-of-contract suit brought by his former employers, the Utah Stars of the ABA.

Chick Hearn said that for the first time Sharman's total concentration was impaired. "If it hadn't affected his coaching," Hearn said, "he wouldn't be a human being. My own son just died, two years ago, at twenty-five years of age, and I know what it means. You try to get away, you try to . . . I don't know, you try to formulate a way to go. His wife had a little girl, and naturally the girl became part of Bill's life. She's gone back to her father, and he felt he had to give up the home they dearly loved. And when they told him at the airport his father had died, he turned to me and said, 'How much more can I take?' "

The obsession with details, the trips to the airport spent hunched forward over the seat just behind the driver, trying to find enough light to read the scouting reports and plan the strategies for the next night's game, all seemed a little less important.

When the longest season had finally ended, I asked Sharman how he had kept his balance with all the shocks. He was cordial, friendly, gifted in the art of public relations, but the strain on his face and in his voice showed. "If someone had told me ahead of time that all of this was going to happen," he said, "it would really have shaken me up. But you never know what life's going to do. I'm not a religious person, but I really feel that everyone is put on earth to be tested. The one thing I kept in mind was something I read someplace: that when you're down keep in mind that life's in a cycle;

things are going to start getting better. It's when you're on top—that's when you've got to be worrying, because things are going to go down.

"When you go through championship pressure as a player, you build up ways of handling anxiety, tension. In a lot of ways, suffering is like that. The worst I ever went through was waiting for the results of Dorothy's . . . you know, she had five operations. In one operation, they were going to go in and depending on where the cancer was, they were going to take off her whole leg and hip. Waiting, and waiting, one operation took five hours. We were in New York, we were in Sloan-Kettering, I think those were the longest five hours of my life, and from there, it just kept getting worse.

"The one good thing in this last year is that basketball moves so quick, there's all this traveling, it keeps my mind occupied. The worst thing you can go through with a personal tragedy is if you have too much free time."

When Sharman talked about the Celtics, he recalled the camaraderie. "Apart from winning the championships, the fun was the best part. Playing cards, listening to Heinsohn's jokes, Russell's laugh . . . You look back, and making friends is the best part."

This wasn't the Sharman one had been taught to expect. After pausing a moment, perhaps he told why: "After the year I've gone through, you begin to look at life a little differently."

Sharman's belief in life cycles seemed to apply, at least in part. In the summer of 1975, after 500 season ticket holders out of 1,500 had canceled, the team announced that Kareem Abdul-Jabbar had been traded to Los Angeles for four Laker players. Within hours of the announcement, more than a hundred people had called in to confess their mistake in canceling, and the Lakers were back as a contender. For Sharman, it was one small consolation after three years of losses—losses of a kind that cannot be dealt with by all the talent and will in the world.

14

Surprises

The achievement of Bill Russell as the centerpiece of the Celtic dynasty was always tarnished by the tension between him and the fans. His outspokenness, his occasional abruptness—outright rudeness at times—and the deeply ingrained racial hostility of a large chunk of the Celtic citizenry made Russell a man apart from the city where he achieved so much glory. It is one of those ironies that no novelist or screenwriter would dare construct that when his playing days were over, he became even more famous than he had been as a player—by virtue of his personality.

By 1969, Russell had been player-coach of the Celtics for three years. His most important coaching asset was the tenacity of his most valuable player—himself—and the maturity and poise of his team. In those three years, at the end of which he was thirty-five years old, he was still averaging forty minutes and more a game, playing in virtually every game, although writers were observing that some of the spring in his legs was gone, and he himself acknowledged that he was relying more on his reputation—on the memory and threat of blocking a rival's shot—than on the deed itself. His teammates, derided as old men after they were trounced by the Philadelphia 76ers in in 1967, were smart enough not to require a high-pressure coach. Sam Jones remained until 1969; Satch Sanders, a wise and experienced veteran, took upon himself the instruction of the younger players; John Havlicek had the tireless body of a machine and the basketball intelligence of a first-rate coach; and players like Bailey Howell and Larry Siegfried were poised players. Both in 1968 and 1969, this poise—and Russell's psychological edge—brought the Celtics championships the dope sheets said they should never have had.

By 1969, however, Russell had had enough. "Everytime I started a game my last year," he told writer Maya Angelou, "I said to myself, 'I've been through this before. I've been playing ball for twenty-five years, and that's enough for anybody.' " He would run down the court and stare at a rivet on the portable court, and wonder how often he had seen that very same rivet, and for minutes at a time he would find his attention wandering, thinking about that rivet, staring at a face in the stands. Over the summer of 1969, with a year left on his contract, he announced his retirement—in an article in *Sports Illustrated.* He told no one, including general manager Auerbach, about his decision.

"I played every game so that at the end of the game, basketball and I would be even," he said later. "And so with the year I quit, I felt even."

It was not a happy leave-taking. The Celtics were angry about his sudden announcement. A restaurant he owned in Boston had gone bankrupt, a Liberian rubber plantation in which he invested collapsed and he had defaulted on a federal loan. A piece of property he owned was seized to pay state and federal taxes. He was separated from his wife and soon divorced.

But Russell had one priceless asset, the same possession that had been such a liability to the Celtic organization: his personality. In 1969, America was a very different place than it had been in 1957, when Russell had begun speaking out about his feelings. Controversy and debate were in the air; blacks were more visible, more militant, and the "shocking" things Russell had once said—about equality of opportunity and discrimination—were now being said by presidential candidates and national commentators. And the college campuses had begun to welcome dissident voices to their communities; indeed, they had begun to pay well for the privilege of hearing unique voices.

The man who withheld so much of himself throughout his playing career began a lecture tour, talking about sports—and about America.

He could flatter his audiences, telling collegians that they were "the greatest generation the world has ever known." And he could gently mock them, telling one audience he would like to say how important this occasion was—"I'd like to, only it wouldn't be true." He could repeat some clichés of the 1960's, wondering why America would put a man on the moon "while right here people are starving and little kids are being bitten by rats."

And he could still shock: at the University of Wisconsin in 1969, he suggested that Wilt Chamberlain had "copped out" in the final playoff game that year by sitting down with an injury for a few moments. "Any injury short of a broken leg or a broken back isn't good enough," he said. "I wouldn't have put him back in the game, either, and I think he's great." This comment ended an amiable off-court relationship between the two rivals.

It was television, however, that gave Russell an audience and a reputation he had never known before. He became the color commentator (one wonders how Russell felt about the title) for the American Broadcasting Company's telecasts of

NBA games, and established himself as one of the most honest and funniest commentators in sportscasting history.

After working one season with Chris Schenkel, Russell was teamed with Keith Jackson, whose quiet competence was a perfect counterpoint to Russell's wit. When Jackson would say that a player was "having a rough game," Russell would say, "No, Keith, he's having a *bad* game." When Jackson asked him what he thought of the Baltimore Bullets' new uniforms, Russell paused for a beat and said "They're *ugly.*" He would watch a slam-dunk and comment dryly, "That's a high-percentage shot." And when a player was belted by a defensive center going to the basket, Russell would repeat his old line from playing days: "You may shoot the free throws, but you may not shoot the lay-ups." Observing Dancing Harry's time-out performance at Madison Square Garden, he noted, "It just goes to prove that not all of us have rhythm." And once when the Lakers' Jim MacMillian was scoring 42 points against Milwaukee, he mistakenly walked toward the Buck bench during a time-out; said Russell: "He's probably gone looking for the guy who's supposed to be guarding him."

He also loved to demystify basketball. "When Red Auerbach put in a new play," Russell said, "it used to take hours, literally hours, to learn the play. Then when the game began, we'd forget it."

Although Russell's commentary ceased when ABC lost the rights to NBA games (CBS gave us Oscar Robertson's breathless swoons at every basket), Russell had become a well-known television personality. He hosted a call-in talk show on a Los Angeles radio station, and gained his widest audience with a series of commercials for Bell Telephone. (This in itself was a fair measure of the different mood of America; the notion that a controversial bearded black should represent Ma Bell to the public would have been satirical in 1957.) In one ad, he was supposed to take a hook shot at a basket while seated at his desk and miss, then explain that the customer could not miss with long distance. Instead, he made the shot—and Russell's cackling laugh of triumph became a part of the commercial. In another, he teamed with Celtic benchwarmer Ron Watts, and the response was so great that the phone company made a sequel.

In 1973, however, Russell was lured back to basketball by Sam Schulman, the owner of the Seattle Supersonics, who had alienated fans by purchasing high-priced players who did not perform and by trading away popular player-coach Lenny Wilkens. The Supersonics crash-landed with a 26–56 record in 1972–73 and Schulman hired Russell as general manager and coach (at a six-figure salary), hoping to retrieve a desperate situation.

Russell immediately applied his own Celtic background to the disorganized, overpriced, underachieving team. He ran a very tough training camp with a lot of drills, a lot of running, and a lot of emphasis on defense. Perhaps his key move was to impose his will on the highly individualistic team—the key commandmant in the Auerbach bible. He increased fines for lateness from a dollar a minute to a hundred dollars a minute, commenting with the words of the farmer who hit a mule over the head with a two-by-four: "You have to get people's attention."

More seriously, he began cutting non-performing players from his roster. John Brisker, $1.3 million contract and all, was demoted to the Eastern League to learn defense. And when he came back, and reporters asked what improvement had been shown, Russell replied that " 'minimal' would be the appropriate word." Brisker soon left the Supersonics, as did Jim McDaniels, no-cut contract notwithstanding. In 1975, Russell even dispatched Spencer Heywood to the New York Knicks for cash.

Russell was a blunt critic of his own team. "We can play any team for three quarters," he said midway through his first season in 1973. "Unfortunately, it's a four-quarter game." And when a friend in Boston said to him, "See you at the playoffs," he responded, "What are you going to do —buy me a ticket?"

His cynicism proved right, but the next year—the 1974–75 season—Seattle began to come together. Like Auerbach, Russell had drafted rookies from winning college teams, and men like Slick Watts began to turn Seattle into a young, quick team. The rookie center, seven-three Jim Burleson, developed into an impressive young player, especially on defense, in the second half of the season. Through tenacity, Seattle got into the playoffs, beat Detroit in the opening round, and took the ultimate champions, Golden State, to six games before being eliminated in the Western semifinals.

Even more remarkable was the public relations effort of Russell's team. The same man who in Boston would not sign autographs sent his players on more than three hundred speaking engagements all over Seattle. Each Monday, the team practiced in a high school gym. The agressive selling paid off: in the 74–75 season, Seattle drew an average of 12,500 people to its regular season games—an average exceeded only by the New York Knickerbockers.

Russell has found in Seattle a city as different from Boston as it is distant. Where he publicly assailed the citizens and writers of Boston during and after his career, he now praises the people of Seattle. "They don't invade my privacy, but they're friendly to me and nice to me. It's one of those places where you don't mind taking a walk because the people just say hello. And that will get you stoned."

Whether Russell will win championships as a coach remains to be seen. It is clear, however, that the times are catching up to him, and suddenly he seems almost in harmony with his surroundings. But it's important to remember that we have changed more than he has. Underneath that friendly exterior, Russell still has the grit that has brought him so far. Summing up his credo, he once told an interviewer, "I try to live my life so that every day I can look a man in the eye and, if I choose, say 'Go to hell.' "

•

Russell's old college roommate, K.C. Jones, never created the stir that Russell had. To the fans and the press, he seemed far less disposed by temperament to become a pro coach, much less a good one. The irony is that he came closer to a championship sooner than Russell himself.

Auerbach had predicted coaching success for K.C. when he signed up as the coach of Brandeis in 1966, saying he was one of the most knowledgeable people ever to play the game. But there were some who doubted his ability to control a team, to direct it according to a philosophy.

Jones's coaching career almost ended as it began, at Brandeis. He had signed to begin coaching the team in the fall of 1966, but stayed with the Celtics an extra year at Auerbach's request, in part because Bill Russell was taking on the coaching chores. When the 1967 season ended, K.C. went to Brandeis, an academically demanding college in the industrial Boston suburb of Waltham. It was not an auspicious three years. Although he put together two straight seasons above .500—the first time Brandeis had achieved such a record—he felt out of place. "It's my fault," Jones said of his confusion. "I assumed college kids would know certain things and they didn't—like pressing, bringing the ball up the court. And there are all those defenses you never see in the pros—the zones, the zone presses, all of that."

Following a 12–14 record in his third season, Jones left Brandeis for an assistant coaching job at Harvard, the school Tom Landers would coach three years later. A year after that, he moved on to Los Angeles, where he assisted former Celtic teammate Bill Sharman with the Lakers. That year,

1971–72, the Lakers put together the single best year of any team in NBA history, winning thirty-three straight games, sixty-nine victories, and a league championship. K.C. Jones was very much a part of that achievement.

It was Sharman's intention to remodel the talent-thick but title-shy Lakers into a Celtic-style team, stressing a running game and a fast break. And Jones had primary responsibility for teaching the fundamentals of defense. He also was the key to Chamberlain's conversion into the rebounding, defensive stalwart.

When K.C. Jones left the Lakers for his first professional head coaching job, a clearer sense of his basic coaching philosophy emerged. Jones, remember, had played nine years under the regimen of Red Auerbach, who proudly boasted of his "dictatorship." He had been a quiet, unprepossessing player, whose biggest run-in with Auerbach came when he was fined for eating pancakes for breakfast—one of Auerbach's pet phobias—and whose biggest flaw was his refusal to tell anyone when he was injured.

But Jones was no acolyte. He was very much his own man, and had his own style of leadership. And when in 1972 he signed on as head coach of the San Diego Conquistadors, the differences between the Auerbach philosophy and K.C. Jones's became clear.

"He treated us like men," Chuck Williams said. "He has a subtle manner. If you are not playing well, he'll ask, 'Is your man too tough? Is he too fast?' You know if you don't respond, you'll go out of the game."

"Years ago, K.C. said, "coaching was a dictatorship. That's all right, but you have to be able to listen as well as talk to the players." In other words, said Jones, the methods that worked for Auerbach simply were not applicable under current conditions. The players entering the pro ranks had lived through the campus turmoil of the 1960's, and through the black pride sentiment of the same era. They were also entering a new competitive climate, in which the existence of two leagues had given the players a freedom of movement they had never had before. And K.C. Jones used his own method of dealing with these changes.

He began at San Diego on a note of surprising success, getting the Q's off to a .500 start. While they did not fulfill that promise, finishing in last place, Jones's coaching abilities brought him to the attention of Abe Pollin, the owner of the Bullets. Despite a talent-rich team that included Elvin Hayes, Wes Unseld, Phil Chenier and Mike Riordan, the Bullets were perennial bridesmaids, making the playoffs only to fall short of title contention. Only once, in 1971, had they gotten past the semifinals, and that year they were humiliated by the Milwaukee Bucks in the finals, losing in four straight games. (The franchise also had a geographical problem, changing from the Baltimore Bullets to the Capitol Bullets to the Washington Bullets in three years; one wag predicted that by the turn of the century they would be the Punta del Este Bullets.)

K.C.'s first year with the Bullets ended with a depressing outcome—a seven-game opening-round playoff loss to the Knicks—but in 1975 it began to come together for the Bullets. They tied with the Celtics for the best regular season record (60-22), then beat the Buffalo Braves in a wearying seven-game series. Then, for the first time, a former member of the Boston Celtics brought a team he was coaching into Boston Garden to meet his former team in the playoffs. The result suggested that someone should have asked Jones to turn in his Secret Manual when he hung up his uniform for the last time.

The Bullets abandoned the offensive rebound and broke back on defense the moment their shots were missed in order to frustrate Boston's fast break. They were at least as successful in frustrating the Celtic defense, which had always begun with pressure on the man bringing the ball upcourt. Jones ran the diminutive Kevin Porter down through the middle, past the slower Boston guards, creating open men all over the court. Cowens was forced out of the middle, and as a consequence Elvin Hayes dominated the center of the court. And K.C.'s Bullets stole a page from the Celtic book by using their bench—Jimmy Jones and Nick Weatherspoon—to ignite the offense when it stalled.

As a result, Boston never got onto its game. The Celtics won two, both achieved without the break and one of them with some last-minute luck. The Bullets won the series in six games, simply blowing Boston off the floor.

The Bullets were not so fortunate in the finals. They were heavily favored over the Golden State Warriors, but the surprising Warriors threw up a ten-man wave which overwhelmed Washington. Ironically, Golden State coach Al Attles used a Celtic-style pressure defense and fast-break offense to win the upset championship in four games.

Despite this loss, the Bullets had demonstrated their capacity to beat the toughest opposition in the league, and once again, just as in San Diego, the players pointed to the attitude of the coach. "I appreciate the way he treats every player as a man," Wes Unseld said. "Unlike some coaches, he is not on an ego trip."

"With another coach," said Elvin Hayes, "this team wouldn't be nearly as good. The whole thing is a reflection of K.C. Jones. He is one of us. He listens to suggestions. The man is just great."

In a little-noticed comment made when he was signed by the Bullets, K.C. Jones gave a clue to his own notion of what makes a good coach. "I come from the Celtics," he said, "which had the greatest philosophy in coaching."

This much was predictable. But then he continued, "Bill Russell's determined way of giving a relaxed attitude to the rest of the players, players helping one another."

It was K.C.'s quiet, understated way of drawing a clear

distinction between himself and the authoritarian style of Red Auerbach; a way of saying that however much one could learn from Auerbach's Celtics, the system and the personal style were subject to revision. Jones's revisionism and his continuing success also suggested that many people—in and out of the Celtic camp—have persistently underestimated the man, first as a player and later as a coach.

•

Indeed, the Celtic spirit appears to affect alumni who never played on a Boston title team. Bob Brannum, the Michigan State star who played four seasons with the Celtics before retiring in 1955, has been coach of Brandeis since 1970. He built a 82–47 record in his first five years, an almost incredible success in a school where academic standards are so high that recruiting is extremely limited and the players' academic work comes first. (One of his prime prospects, with high potential but low achievement, was put in a special remedial program. The boy graduated in three years—depriving Brannum of one year's worth of talent.)

Even without the luxury of great talent, Brannum installed the pressure defense and the fast-break game he learned under Auerbach—not only as a player but also as a staff aide at Auerbach's basketball camp and at the Celtics' rookie and training camps.

"I remember once hearing Red make a substitution," Brannum says. "The guy asked Red, 'What did I *do?*'

" 'Nothing,' Red said. 'That's why you're out.'

"So if a kid is in there for five or eight minutes, and he hasn't made his rebounds or taken any shots, I get somebody in there who's going to be doing something. It doesn't even have to be right—but he *has* to be doing something."

Brannum is constantly applying the famous "sixth man" theory created by Auerbach. "I try very hard to go along with the sixth- or seventh-man thing Red started," he says. "And, like Red always says, I want my substitute to be *better* when he comes into the game than the guy he replaces. That's the attitude he always looked for; get the guy who can come off the bench and be going one hundred percent when he crosses the line. There are starters who are worth their weight in gold as starters, but who wouldn't be worth a damn coming off that bench. They just aren't there.

15

The Collegians

The influence of the Celtic men is not confined to pro basket-ball; it extends into the college ranks, particularly in and around the Boston area. Despite the failure of the Celtics to draw large crowds, their partisans were loyal, and many players felt a genuine affection for the region. Bob Cousy settled in nearby Worcester and started his coaching at Boston College; K.C. Jones began at Brandeis, in the suburb of Waltham; Tom Sanders coached across the river at Harvard; Jim Loscutoff settled in at Boston State College; and Bob Brannum, a player of the pre-dynasty era, succeeded K.C. Jones at Brandeis. These ex-Celtics, in contrast to those who entered pro coaching, worked without top talent and largely without recognition. They did not lead big-time teams with national ranking and big-tournament possibilities. Their success in making lesser teams into winners suggests something important about the Celtic approach. It is not limited to the higher levels of the game but works wherever there are two teams and a basketball.

distinction between himself and the authoritarian style of Red Auerbach; a way of saying that however much one could learn from Auerbach's Celtics, the system and the personal style were subject to revision. Jones's revisionism and his continuing success also suggested that many people—in and out of the Celtic camp—have persistently underestimated the man, first as a player and later as a coach.

"It's very hard to sell that. My last year in Sheboygan [1950–51], I was scoring twenty points a game, and when I got to Boston my ass got parked on the bench and Bones McKinney was starting. But Red knew how to make a bench person part of the team, and he paid you for what you contributed teamwise. You don't need a twenty-point-per-game average to get a raise with him. If you pay a man what a starter's getting, he's got no squawk. Here, I try to make my bench know how important they are."

Then, of course, there are the two Auerbach essentials: the fast break and tough defense. "We run like hell here," says Brannum. "Or at least we try to. It's the way to play the game—the only way. Why is John Havlicek so efficient? Because you can't ever *find* the son of a bitch. He's running, running, running. It's hard enough just to run with him, just to take as many steps, let alone play defense against him. So I take my kids and tell them, 'If somebody's running, you can't defense him, you can't help out, because you're running so hard.' On defense, we trap the other guys, we try and disrupt. People who watch us think we aren't organized, because we have these crazy trap plays. But we know what we're doing."

Brannum has not applied all of Auerbach's style to his coaching career. He readily acknowledges that the academic orientation of his players, and the different era, make the authoritarian approach all but inapplicable. But, he says, "they know who runs this team."

And Brannum remains close to the Celtics and to Auerbach. "When I walk in," he says, "it's like old home week —for any of the old guys. I've gone to Red a couple of times with a problem, and he's terrific. He'll give you a bunch of shit when you tell him you want to talk with him—'What the hell is it? Jesus, I haven't got the time'—but then he'll sit and listen and he's terrific.

"You know what the thing about Red was? He wouldn't

let you lose. You might get beat, but you didn't lose. I can't tell you what he said or did, or what it was—just, you didn't lose."

•

Jim Loscutoff, a nine-year Celtic veteran, has coached for the last nine years at Boston State College, and his teams have won—two games out of every three. For Loscutoff, the most important lesson from his Celtic years has to do with *will.*

I asked Loscutoff what, if any, of the Auerbach philosophy he had put to use at Boston State. He thought a moment.

"A way to win," he said finally. "Red's basic philosophy is: if you're going to play the game, play the game to win, and play it as hard as you possibly can. Every kid who makes my team, if he doesn't bust his ass in a game situation, he's wasting my time, and he's wasting his time. I'd rather have a kid give me a hundred and twenty percent than a kid who's really talented giving me seventy-five percent.

"I have a way that I think encourages that. I play every kid on my ball club. I may play thirteen kids in a game, even if it's a tight game, a close game, 'cause they're going to bust their ass. I could hurt my team, but I haven't so far."

But isn't that a contradiction of the "win-at-all-costs" idea?

"I think I would do the same thing as a pro coach," Loscutoff said. "My feeling would be that these guys are getting top dollar, and if they don't bust their ass, I'd be in a situation to trade them or get rid of them for somebody who wants to work. A prime example is the Van Arsdale brothers. If I was a coach, and had a way to grab both of them, I'd do it. Dave Cowens is the same way. So is Paul Silas. It's the hungry instinct. That's where the Celtics have it over a lot of other clubs.

"Look," he said. "The kids are here because they want to play the game. And I have nothing to offer them. Maybe if

I was at a major college with five, six, seven scholarships a year to offer, I'd have more of a hold on them, like saying, 'If you kids don't play, I'm gonna take your scholarships away.' But I don't like that. I'd hate it. I like the situation I'm in right now because the kids are here because they want to play. I don't care if they smoke, drink beer—maybe a team that drinks beer together wins together.

"Sure, coaching is an egotistical business. I ask myself, jeez, how would I do at a school like Indiana or UCLA? In 1975, I even applied for the Stanford job. That's my home. But I couldn't afford to go there. And I didn't like the situation. I'm happy with what I'm doing now. I have a camp thing, and I enjoy working with kids five, six, seven, watching their faces."

I watched Loscutoff talk with a prospective young player, a playmaking high school guard. There was no pressure, no promise save the chance to play a lot, and an invitation to drop by the end-of-the-year party for the team at Loscutoff's home where there'd be pizza, wine and beer.

It was decidedly soft-sell, and yet it suggested that one could create a winning attitude without encountering the temptations that drove a Bob Cousy out of college coaching. Somehow, Loscutoff had managed to put aside the high-pressure world of professional athletics without sacrificing the winning attitude that is so much a part of the Celtics.

•

Other former Bostonians have not been as fortunate. Tom "Satch" Sanders took over as head coach at Harvard University in 1973, fully recognizing that at Harvard basketball was a "minor-minor." The capacity of the ancient gymnasium was barely 1,400; the Harvard basketball team had never won an Ivy League title.

In his first three years, Sanders compiled a 31–42 record, spotted by occasional "big wins" over Cincinnati and Boston

College. The team labored under some unusual handicaps: for example, when the Radcliffe varsity used the main court in the Indoor Athletic Building, the Harvard team was shunted to the side court—where, as one observer described it, "it's bring-your-flashlight time." Despite such handicaps, however, one Harvard official notes, "We think he's the guy who'll put us back into Ivy League contention."

Sanders himself is committed to the notion that college athletics cannot supersede the academic function. As he said when he took over the job, "I have seen too many men go from college into pro ball and last maybe a year. When they are cut—and so many are cut—they are through. Where can they go? Only back home. They have finished college without going to college."

•

The unhappiest experience in the collegiate coaching ranks belongs to former offensive standout Sam Jones. Jones retired after the 1969 season—the last season of the dynasty years—to take a job as basketball coach and athletic director at Federal City College in Washington, D.C. The job was obtained through the help of a long-time, if part-time, resident of Washington, Red Auerbach. Jones was a popular figure in Boston, and his retirement was marked by a "Sam Jones" day at Boston Garden with a city council proclamation and a gift of a partial payment on a new home for the Jones family in Washington. The job seemed perfect: Sam Jones had a quietly effective manner, and demonstrated a concern for the inner-city black youths that Federal City College was designed to serve. In fact, while still playing in Boston he had discovered a Roxbury boy at Boston Trades Vocational High School and paid his tuition to the Laurinburg Institute in North Carolina. The boy was Jimmy Walker.

But, like so many other ideas of the 1960's, Federal City College had more good intentions than hard-nosed efficiency. First, forty-seven football players were found academically ineligible; the sport was dropped. Jones gave up his basketball coaching to concentrate on running the athletic department. Then, in 1973, he left Federal City College to become basketball coach at his old alma mater, renamed North Carolina Central University.

After he left Federal City, an audit of the athletic department showed some $4,000 in money had been spent outside "normal" channels. This was not a case of anyone getting rich; rather, this small, new school catering to poor kids was, in a small way, emulating the practices of its academic elder brothers. The athletic department had paid $54 in parking tickets for athletes, and $121 had been spent in personal loans to them. The school had paid $185 for a lifetime membership in TWA's Ambassador Club. And Jones had bought a home, then leased it to the athletic department for $800 a month to be rented out to athletes. Hardly Watergate stuff, but enough to cloud his tenure.

His return to North Carolina was no happier, though for different reasons. After one 5–16 season, the strain of running a team on a total budget of $14,000 was too great, and in the summer of 1974 he quit his job by telegram. A few months later, he became assistant coach of the NBA New Orleans Jazz, but after the 1974–75 season he left that job. He is thus far the only Celtic of the dynasty years who has coached without a winning season. If only by contrast, that fact illustrates the remarkable record of ex-Celtics who have gone into coaching, regardless of the prominence of the team they joined.

16

The Holdovers

The continuity that Red Auerbach brought to the Boston Celtics was not confined to management and style of play. It extended as well to the players. More than any other professional team, the Celtics put a remarkable number of the same players on the floor year after year. Cousy and Russell stayed for thirteen years apiece; Sharman, Sam Jones and Sanders for ten; Loscutoff, Ramsey and K.C. Jones for nine. Even after the dynasty ended, this tradition of continuity was maintained, principally through the inspired play of two men. One of them was extraordinarily gifted and used his talent to the hilt. The other survived as a Celtic by putting his more limited skills to the best possible use. Seven years after the last dynasty team, they were both still at work for the Celtics.

•

For John Havlicek, the collapse of the Celtic dynasty was a special burden. With Sam Jones and Bill Russell gone, and

Satch Sanders injured, Havlicek became an instant elder statesman, and he realized only gradually how heavy the responsibility was to be.

"There's no question about it," Auerbach says. "He did all of it, he took the entire leadership role on the court and off . . . to the point where it hurt him a little bit for a while, because he was so concerned with what everybody else was doing that his own game was neglected."

Without Sam Jones, Havlicek took on the offensive burden, increasing his average to more than 24 points a game in 1969–70, then to 28.9 points the year after that. For those three years, Havlicek was also the team's top playmaker, the team's best foul shooter, and—in the interval between Russell and Dave Cowens—the team's leading *rebounder*. (The rebounding statistics show how badly the Celtics missed a big man: Russell had never averaged less than 19.3 rebounds in his career; in 1969–70, Havlicek led the team with a 7.8 average.)

"Even though I had my best scoring years," Havlicek said, long after the Celtics had risen again to the top of the league, "they were the most frustrating for me." In part, this frustration stemmed from the fact that from his high school days on, Havlicek had always played for a winning team. His Ohio State team reached the NCAA finals three years in a row, and the Celtics won NBA championships six times in Havlicek's first seven years. Celtic legend has it that when Havlicek's predecessor, Frank Ramsey, lost his first game as a pro, he was incredulous; he had played on a Kentucky team that, in his senior year, never lost a game. Havlicek, too, was accustomed to winning, to championships. The fact that the Celtics in 1970 played under .500 ball and didn't qualify for the playoffs was all but incomprehensible to him.

Something else about that year, and the disappointing though steadily improving years that followed, sheds some light on Havlicek's character. Havlicek's public personality had been about as contentious as a Quaker at meeting. But now he actually began criticizing his teammates and—indirectly—Coach Heinsohn for the team's erratic and inconsistent play. He was no fan of Heinsohn's courtside antics and temper tantrums—and the technical fouls they cost the Celtics. And he chastised the younger players for their "dumb" behavior in failing to remember the simple Celtic patterns.

For John Havlicek is a thoroughly methodical man; he appears to live his life the way he plays—without quirks, without sudden bursts of brilliance or moments of indifference, but with a relentless, almost unnerving consistency. (He is, in this sense, a throwback to Bill Sharman, albeit without the fanaticism that characterized Sharman's career.) He is a careful, prudent list-maker of men, whose habits are as carefully planned as his mealtimes.

"You would not enjoy eating with him," says Bob Wolf, his long-time friend and one-time attorney. "He will put his knife over here, and his fork over here, and ver-r-ry slow-w-wly cut each piece exactly just so." In the locker room, he takes off his clothes and stores them in exactly the same order everytime. He has been known to check out new hotels in NBA cities, and to recommend the better ones to the Celtics. There is a blueprint for everything.

"The one thing he can't stand is stupidity," Wolf says, and for Havlicek the Celtics of the first post-Russell years simply did not play smart basketball.

"Pure and simple mental mistakes that don't really require a great deal of thinking are things that upset me the most on a basketball court," Havlicek says. "Because the teams that are winning are the people that eliminate mistakes." He was the kind of player who would spend hours after a painful defeat in a parking lot outside an arena with his teammates, reviewing the patterns and the assignments, trying to figure out what went wrong.

Havlicek was the key transitional figure between dynasty and rebuilding. In attempting to keep alive the traditions of the winning years, he and fellow veterans Don Nelson and Tom Sanders reminded the younger players of the longstanding traditional dress code (jackets and ties or turtlenecks), so that the players would feel a link to the past. And it was Havlicek who expressed dissatisfaction with Coach Heinsohn's refusal to drill the patterns into the heads of the younger players.

There are those who simply cannot credit Havlicek's expressions of belief in the Celtic traditions of team play and unselfishness. His life, too, appears almost too good to be true. He is married to a beautiful blond former high school cheerleader sweetheart, an enthusiastic supporter of charities and good works, a non-smoking, non-swearing believer who spends a few minutes each day reading a chapter from an inspirational book called *The Inner Room.* But as deeply as any questioner can discern, Havlicek's life and beliefs are for real.

"There are times," he said one day in the Celtics' offices, "when I think the league is weaker than it was many years ago. Fundamentally, I think the teams were much better. They're more *exciting* today because of the abilities of people, but the teams of the Celtic past, I think, probably understood the game on a higher level than the last [1974] world championship team we had." It is the dive-under-the-press-table-after-a-loose-ball style of play, rather than the startling, leaping, one-on-one style of many of today's players, that is Havlicek's measure of achievement.

His own, unglamorously consistent style of play made him the floor leader, captain and symbolic leader of the Celtics throughout the post-Russell years. By 1973, he was important enough to receive the highest contract ever given a Celtic—$700,000 over three years—and he turned down a blanket offer from the ABA for $1.2 million to play anywhere, in any city he chose. In 1974, he finally proved to the country what NBA players and Celtic fans had long known: that he was a superstar.

In a playoff series against the Buffalo Braves, it was Havlicek, playing in the backcourt, who helped build the lead that decided the sixth and final game. Against the Knicks—who had beaten Boston in 1973 only after Havlicek separated his shoulder—he scored from 25 to 36 points in each of the five games, hitting on forty-one shots out of seventy. And against Milwaukee in the finals, Havlicek put on a sensational performance. In the two-overtime sixth game, he scored 9 of Boston's 11 overtime points. He was named Most Valuable Player in the playoffs, and (the final measure of success for a Celtic) Boston won the championship. John Havlicek lacked the flair that has made other superstars famous. But his ceaseless movement, his deceptively quick release of a jump shot, his passes to the open teammate, his defensive pressure on opponents—all these unspectacular talents—suggest that greatness in a team sport consists of doing the things that make your team win. That is the central point to his achievement—and the Celtics' as well.

•

For Don Nelson, the man who had been cut by the Lakers in 1965, who had sweated through days of uncertainty before Red Auerbach called to invite him to a tryout, the rebuilding years gave him the chance to find his niche—that of a slow but steady offensive player who could be counted on to provide scoring power and court stability. On a team that had lost its key offensive and defensive players in the same year, stability was an urgent necessity. And Don Nelson was there, from the rebuilding through his retirement after the 1975–76 season, to provide just that quality.

Not that the press—or Nelson, for that matter—ever recognized him as a player of great value. He was convinced he would be traded in the spring of 1971. Again, in January of 1974, he said, "If they had the expansion draft right away, I don't think the Celtics would protect me." Yet Don Nelson, in his own way, personified one key to the team's enduring success; he was a player who took his ability to the absolute limit, and who learned to live within his limits.

A computer ranking of professional basketball players might well put Don Nelson near the bottom. He had no speed and limited mobility, and he once lost one-on-one a contest with a sportswriter (roughly equivalent to losing a memory contest to an amnesiac). He shot fouls in a manner designed to give a high school coach cardiac shock, balancing the ball in the cup of his right hand, pushing it toward the basket like a shot-putter. But a computer does not measure the capacity of a bsketball player to steady a team that is losing its offensive poise, or to provide a basket when neither the fast break nor the pattern offense is working. A computer does not measure the brains that allow a six-foot-six forward to play the pivot against Kareem Abdul-Jabbar and actually contain him for an entire game. A computer does not measure the capacity of a player to bend the rules —with a cagey hand on a shirt or a wrist—and drive an opponent to distraction. (One of the less explosive members of the New York Knickerbockers told newsmen that Nelson is one opponent he would like to fight.)

There is one fact about Nelson that even a computer might appreciate: he was the best shooter on the Boston Celtics. Five times he led the team in shooting percentage from the floor. His .508 percentage in the 1974 championship year was the second best in Celtic history (only Bailey Howell did better, in 1967). He was unspectacular but deadly, throwing up fifteen-foot one-handers with a flick of the wrist and a quick release. The shots weren't fancy or breath-taking, but a lot of them went in the basket.

When Willis Reed ran into a Boston reporter before the start of the Knick-Celtic Eastern final that year, he asked, "How's Nelson?" The reporter asked why he wanted to know. "Because he's one of the very best shooters in the league," Willis replied. "I'd just as soon not see him in the playoffs." In the playoffs, Nelson hit 11.4 points per game, playing less than half of the time, and shot an even .500.

Coach Heinsohn said of Nelson's shooting, "A guy can be right on him, and he will sense the moment when this man will react. All he needs is half an inch to get his shot off, because he has such economy of motion. He is a finger and body shooter. There is no arm in his shot at all. The body gives him direction—twenty-five feet with a flick of the wrist." In the 1974–75 season, the wrist flicked better than ever; Nelson averaged 14 points during the season, and his .539 field goal percentage set an all-time Celtic record. At the time, Don Nelson was almost thirty-five years old.

It was easy to underestimate Nelson on the court; in fact, the basketball world was littered with the bleaching bones of rookies who saw Don Nelson's slow gait and assumed the veteran could be blown off the court by a faster, younger man. "He takes those young leapers and makes their strength work against them," Heinsohn said. And his shrewd head and shoulder fakes brought him endless trips to the free-throw line.

It was also easy to underestimate Nelson off the court. He is a pleasant-faced, blond man with the placid features of a cornfed Midwesterner, and more than one observer has been fooled into painting Nelson as some modern, urbanized American Gothic. In fact, Nelson is both smarter and more complicated than a first impression suggests. Auerbach has said, "Don makes the most of his God-given talents—more so than any athlete I've ever seen."

He is, first of all, blunt about his limits. "The sixth man is generally a better player than the fifth man," Nelson said in 1975. "Silas is certainly a better player than I am; there's no way you can get around that. He's not as good a shooter, but he's a better rebounder, a better passer, a better defensive player. Paul had the starter job, and he gave it up because

I'm at the age now where I have trouble getting off the bench. And the fact that Silas gave it up clearly prolonged my career. There aren't very many teams that have guys who would do that." His head and shoulder fakes are, in his eyes, as much a product of what he can no longer do as what he does well. "I used to have a real quick first step to the hoop," he said. "I don't have that any more, so I use more fakes to get to the hoop now. A veteran must adjust his game. You can't get away with the same things year after year no matter if you're as quick as you once were or not."

When Nelson broke Tom Sanders' "ironman" record, playing in 465 straight games despite a chronically painful Achilles tendon, he said simply, "I'm from the old school. I believe you're paid and should be on the job. I have a certain role on this club, and if I'm not here then it hurts the overall function." Nelson, more than most contemporary professional basketball players, had a sense of obligation. In an era when more and more players were begged to join a team, Nelson was of an era and a set of circumstances in which the line between professional success and oblivion was very thin indeed. When he was asked, jestingly, about playing with the NBA All-Stars, he said lightly, "Oh, I wouldn't look that bad. I'd stop at one end of the court and wait for the ball to come down. That way they'd never mind my lack of speed."

Nelson also possessed of a clear understanding of an athlete's fragility. He was a compulsive worker in the off-season; a local advertising representative for a basketball publication; operator of a camp; a highly successful promoter of exhibition basketball games. By carefully picking cities where professional teams do not play, Nelson managed to draw remarkable crowds for pre-season games. In the fall of 1974, the first match-up between Kareem Abdul-Jabbar and Bill Walton drew a gate of $70,000 in Dayton, Ohio. Nelson spent thirty-two straight days in Dayton to assure the success of the Milwaukee-Portland match-up. Before the end of the 1975 season, he said there wouldn't be a free moment in his summer schedule. And when I asked him why he pushed himself so hard, he said without emotion, "In my own mind, I only have a certain number of years where I can make what I call easy money. Even though I have to work harder than Havlicek for it, it's still easy money."

Nelson shared with many Celtics a competitive drive that takes its toll on his peace of mind. He rejected the kind of mental "psyching process" that Bob Cousy used to go through, working up a ferocious hatred of his current opponents—"I think that's all bullshit"—but the calm façade is very misleading.

"I don't show my emotions, but I have plenty of them," he said the night before a critical game against the Washington Bullets in the 1975 playoffs. "I don't sleep very good at night; I was up most of last night. When I did sleep, I was soaking wet. The bed smelled terrible. The sheets, everything was soaked. I guess people think I don't have emotions because I don't show many emotions on the court or anywhere, but I'm up real tight. When the ball goes up, that particular thing goes away."

Of his benefactor Auerbach, Nelson says, "He's gotta be my buddy no matter what he does to me, because he gave me the chance. He's one of the few guys where you have a conception of how good he was supposed to be, and when I got there my value of him went up even more.

"It wasn't so much his technical knowledge of the game. It was more his ability at handling people. He did that better than anybody I've ever known. I've read a lot about Lombardi, and they've got to be cut from the same mold."

It has been an uneven career for Nelson. At first, working as a back-up forward to Tom Sanders and Willie Naulls, he seemed an afterthought. But in the first shocking post-Russell season, Nelson became a leader, playing at forward and occasionally at center. ("He's our best pivot man," Heinsohn said, by way of indicting the play of Henry Finkel and Jim "Bad News" Barnes.) Nelson averaged 15.4 points a game—his career high—and provided an element of stability to the decimated team. And after an operation in 1973 to relieve a chronic leg injury, he came into his own at the age of thirty-three. As with earlier Celtics, he was not pressured into attempting the jobs he could not do. No one demanded that Nelson fight for rebounds, or lead the break; instead, his job was to start the game, provide a steady offensive power, and then retire in favor of the speed and muscle of Paul Silas.

Nelson has made this limited but crucial role his own. As late as the 1975 playoffs, his shooting ability was a prime factor in Boston's five-game rout of the Houston Rockets. And twice in the Eastern final against the Washington Bullets, Nelson had a hot hand in the first half—only to be denied the ball in the second. By the time Nelson announced his retirement in late 1975, he ranked fifth among all NBA playoff performers in floor shooting, and he had become "the old pro"—a familiar role on the Celtic team. He helped bring along newer players, teaching them the habits that have made the Celtics winners.

Now it is time for a new career. Listening to a country-rock guitarist, I asked Nelson how much of his shooting ability he'd give up to play a guitar like that, and he laughingly said, "All of it." Whatever his future holds, Nelson has made his past secure. From uncertainty and limitations, he fashioned a basketball career that should put his number on the banner high in the rafters of the Boston Garden, another exemplar of the Celtic adage that winning teams are made up of players who can make intense and intelligent use of commonplace skills.

17

The Stepchild Stays On

When Tom Heinsohn took over the Celtics' coaching job in the late summer of 1969, following the sudden retirement of player-coach Bill Russell, he was facing an impossible task. He got the job because he was familiar with the Celtic style of play, and because he was, in contrast to other candidates, both available and willing. He had only days to prepare before the rookies reported to camp.

In retrospect, Heinsohn performed admirably. His team played under .500 ball for only one year; in his third year, they were a playoff team; in his fourth, division champions. And in his fifth year, they were NBA champions once again. Heinsohn was named Coach of the Year in 1974 for his achievement.

But there are some men who are doomed to be deprived of the thing they most want and deserve. And in Heinsohn's case, that something seems to be fair measure of respect. The Celtics are still widely viewed as Red Auerbach's team. Heinsohn's players often criticize him uninhibitedly to the press. And he himself—one of the smartest people ever to play basketball—seems to feed this disrespect, both by his on-the-court conduct and by off-the-court attempts to prove his worth.

His behavior on the court, for example, was—or should have been—an embarassment to any grown-up adult. He chain-smoked cigarettes; he leapt up from the bench every few seconds; he stared out at the court balefully; he sulked like a four-year-old child who has had a lollipop taken from him. He is one of the few people I have ever seen turn purple —literally—and he was capable of finishing a temper tantrum with a complete midair twist of his body.

In his determination to prove that he is his own man, he sometimes hurt himself. In the spring of 1975, angered by a *Christian Science Monitor* report that Auerbach was still the brains behind the Celtics, Heinsohn wrote an angry letter to the paper.

"I'm tired of reading and hearing all the time that Tom Heinsohn doesn't really coach the Boston Celtics . . . It isn't true, and what's more I can prove it.

"We use the fast break," he continued, "but execute it in a vastly different manner than was done in the Bob Cousy, Russell, Auerbach era. Our current fast break was designed by me, necessitated by the fact that we have only a six-eight center, and no longer have the awesome rebounding talents of Mr. Russell.

"We still use the Celtics' famous Six Plays, with options, that Auerbach developed years ago. But they have been modified by me to fit our current personnel and team defenses. We also rely heavily on two pattern offenses not used in the Auerbach regime and developed entirely by me."

To many Celtic veterans and observers, however, this is more rationalization than reality. Basketball is not nuclear physics, and a fast-break, pressure-defense philosophy does not require technical genius to implement. When the Celtics

—under Auerbach or Heinsohn—lacked the talent on the court to win, coaching philosophy did not work. When the Celtics possessed the strong center, the playmaking and shooting guards, they won. Moreover, the Auerbach philosophy and the Auerbach draft choices dominated the Celtic comeback as they had originally dominated the Celtic dynasty.

For Heinsohn, a proud, intelligent, combative personality, this subordination to a more powerful personality rankled. And in the eyes of some it made him obsessed with proving his worth.

One of his old friends and teammates, Jim Loscutoff, says, "Tommy and I are the greatest friends in the world. But if we'd sit down, and I'd say, 'Tommy, here's an offense that I used here in college that might work,' he'd say, 'No way. Might work in college, but in *pro* ball . . .' He'd always bring that in, 'in *pro* ball it would never work.' In the last two years, I have never discussed basketball with him. It's like talking to Jesus Christ."

Heinsohn is not, however, simply a man with arrested emotional development. He is reacting to a depressing fact —that Tom Heinsohn as a coach has been as underrecognized as Tom Heinsohn the player. Just as his role as a Celtic, his treatment at the hands of Auerbach, earned him less than he deserved as a player, so the impossible position he took on as coach of the Celtics under Auerbach deprived him of his due as a coach. The stepchild has remained the stepchild.

Heinsohn had built a highly successful career as an insurance salesman and executive after his retirement in 1965, and he stayed close to the team as a television broadcaster as well, working with Auerbach after he left coaching in what must have been the most hopelessly biased duo in broadcast history.

When Auerbach quit the coaching job in 1966, Heinsohn was one of those approached about taking over. He turned down the offer, as he later explained, because "Russell was still playing, and I knew I couldn't handle Russell. I knew nobody was going to handle Russell, so I said to Red, 'Why don't you make Russell the coach? He's got so much damn pride he'll handle himself.' "

Three years later, in the wake of Russell's sudden retirement, Heinsohn took over the coaching reins under the most inauspicious conditions imaginable.

With Coach Russell gone, the Celtics' most potent weapon was gone also—Russell the Center. The psychological edge, the presence of a man who was a legend to many of the younger NBA players, disappeared from the middle of Boston's line-up. Now other teams could challenge the middle without fear in their hearts. And the key to Boston's winning fast break—the big, rebound-grabbing center—was gone. Asking Heinsohn to coach Boston without Russell was like asking a director to stage *Hamlet* without the Prince. Neither Henry Finkel nor Jim "Bad News" Barnes had the capacity to perform as a Celtic center must.

To make matters worse, Russell's retirement had caught Auerbach totally off-guard. He had drafted Jo Jo White first in the 1969 draft, to provide some youthful firepower in the backcourt, because he was sure he would not be needing a new center for a while. Russell had a year left on his contract, and in the past Auerbach had been able to persuad veterans to stay on after their intended retirements. Both Cousy and K.C. Jones had remained an extra year, and Auerbach had apparently been confident he could persuade Russell to play beyond the expiration date of his contract, too. "I'll always feel Russell quit too soon," he told a reporter after the decision was made. "He could have been outstanding for three more years. He had brains for the game; he could have finessed his way through."

Russell's departure broke the continuity that had always blessed the Celtics. Throughout the winning years, Auerbach had brought replacements along slowly, taking the Jones boys to replace Cousy and Sharman, working Havlicek in as Ramsey's replacement, and letting veterans like Carl Braun, Gene Conley, Andy Phillip, Arnie Risen and Bailey Howell contribute their knowledge and poise to the team while younger players worked their way in. Had Russell played for two or three more years, Auerbach might well have preserved the dynasty intact—by drafting a big man in 1970, and giving him a year or two to learn under Russell. Instead, Tom Heinsohn's first year of coaching was spent picking up pieces.

Sam Jones retired at the same time as Russell. His departure took away a powerful scoring weapon—Jones had averaged more than 20 points a game in four of his last five seasons. Tom Sanders was slowed by injuries. That left John Havlicek as the grizzled veteran, and a handful of other experienced players: Don Nelson, Larry Siegfried, Bailey Howell. It was not a championship team.

The New York Knicks, who had been NBA doormats so long that their uniforms should have said WELCOME on them, finally put together a winning team in 1970 while the Celtics languished. And when the Knicks started to become winners, New York—a basketball town to its roots—went beserk.

"We won eleven championships and had one book written about us," Auerbach growled after the Knicks won the title. "The Knicks won one championship and had eleven books written about them." The numbers may have been off, but the sentiments were undeniably accurate. So the Celtics were subjected to the added humiliation of yielding the championship to a team that got far more recognition for a year's achievement than the Celtics had gotten in ten.

All this may have been good for basketball. But for Heinsohn, who had played on winning teams all of his life and missed a championship only once in his nine years as a player, the situation was impossible. In that first season, his bench antics frequently cost the Celtics technical fouls and points in the closing moments of tight games. Often he would cast glances over at the press bench, where Red Auerbach sat, as if to seek approval for his version of the Old Master's referee baiting. But Auerbach at least seemed to have a purpose in his antics. With Heinsohn, the rage seemed uncontrolled. "He really was a raving maniac that first year," a long-time member of the Celtics' family remembered. "He was compensating for what he didn't know about the game as a coach. It got so bad, Havlicek was thinking seriously about looking to get traded."

Heinsohn's behavior improved slightly in succeeding years. And the record of the team shows that once again Heinsohn was perhaps underestimated. Even granting Auerbach's dominant role in drafting the talent and administering the team, it is clear that Heinsohn, too, contributed to the rebuilding. As Heinsohn grew more comfortable in his role, Auerbach withdrew from day-to-day supervision. After that first season, he moved from the press bench up into the stands, across from the Celtic bench (although some people insisted that Auerbach had devised a set of hand signals to coach the team). Instead of attending ten practices a year, he cut it down to five, then to showing up only when he was asked about specific problems. And he backed Heinsohn's authority completely.

In the 1969–70 season, for example, Larry Siegfried and Em Bryant openly challenged Heinsohn. Tommy wanted to use the break; Bryant and Siegfried insisted that without a dominant, rebounding center, a slow, pattern offense—the kind the Knicks were using—was more appropriate. After that season, both Bryant and Siegfried were taken in the expansion draft (Bryant signed on briefly as assistant coach of Seattle under Bill Russell; Siegfried became assistant coach of the Houston Rockets).

Auerbach stood solidly with Heinsohn. "We broke Siegfried in to be a leader," Auerbach said, "and he couldn't
accept it. Then he thought he knew more than Tommy and
he began to question him." Auerbach was accustomed to
being the unquestioned "dictator" in his coaching days, and
he was willing to give the new coach similar powers over the
players. "I'm not running a union here," he used to say.

And year by year the Celtics regained their touch. Boston
writers and fans, used to seeing championships arrive with
the regularity of spring, talked about the long drought, the
decline of the Celtics. But by any fair standard, the drought
lasted only one year.

In 1970–71, with backcourt men Jo Jo White and Don
Chaney gaining confidence, and with rookie center Dave
Cowens ripping backboards off their supports in his ferocious
pursuit of rebounds, Boston finished with a 44-38 record,
barely missing the playoffs. The next year, they finished with
a 56-26 record, winning their division for the first time since
1965. They beat Atlanta in six games, but lost to the Knicks
in five games.

By 1972–73, the Celtics were once again one of the best
teams in the NBA. Their regular-season record of 68-14, best
in the history of the franchise, earned Dave Cowens the
league's MVP award, and Heinsohn was named Coach of the
Year. And the Celtics missed the NBA finals only because
John Havlicek, the captain and offensive sparkplug of the
team, was injured during the Eastern final against New York.
Still, the Celtics held on until the Knicks finally, mercilessly,
exploited Havlicek's injury to win the seventh game.

Yet Heinsohn's coaching capacity was the subject of open
doubt, even among the players. Some of them questioned the
endless, minutely drawn x's and o's that were supposed to
cover every possible situation on the court, and which were
frequently ignored when play began. Havlicek and Nelson
were publicly concerned that the Celtic offense was too pre-

dictable. Paul Silas commented, "One of the things that surprised me when I came here was that you didn't need strong leadership to win."

Even the final affirmation of the worth of any coach—an NBA championship—did not win for Heinsohn his full deserts. In the 1973–74 season, Boston breezed to another Division crown. Then, in the finals, they faced the Milwaukee Bucks, who were led by the single most intimidating force in the game: Kareem Abdul-Jabbar.

For six games, Boston and Milwaukee exchanged strategic moves. Heinsohn had said long ago, "Basketball is chess on the run; I am involved in a thinking man's game." This series, one of the most fascinating in NBA history, proved it. No team won two games in a row—in each game the losing coach adjusted to the strategy that had worked against his team in the previous game. In the end, the Celtics beat Abdul-Jabbar by using the one weapon against him that they had deliberately set aside for the first six games.

The Celtics had refused to collapse on Jabbar, preferring to let Cowens play him man-to-man. Cowens had done as good a job as possible, but with the deciding game coming up, a hot night by Jabbar, guarded only by Cowens, would make a Milwaukee victory likely. This prospect was on the minds of Heinsohn, assistant coach John Killilea and Bob Cousy as they sat in Red Auerbach's office before the seventh game and talked tactics.

Cousy asked about the possibility of Cowens fronting Jabbar, trying to play between him and the ball. And Killilea and Heinsohn agreed that that strategy would not be enough. They agreed that other players, Paul Silas in particular, would position themselves between the big man and the basket while Cowens stayed in front. That left one question: Who would guard the Bucks' Cornell Warner?

"Nobody," Heinsohn said. "I am going to give Cornell Warner a chance to achieve greatness." The result: Warner took no advantage of the opening, scoring one point in twenty-nine minutes; Jabbar was held scoreless for a full quarter; and Boston won the game 102–87 to bring the NBA title back to Boston.

It was a brilliant strategy, and it paid off. Did Heinsohn finally gain recognition for his own intelligence? The next day one sports page headline read: COUSY STRATEGY SAVES CELTICS. Once again, Heinsohn was haunted by the Ghost of Celtics Past.

18

Last Thoughts

The official explanation says that the value of sports is in its lessons of competition, preparing young people for the rigors of life. But the story of the Boston Celtic dynasty and the apparent durability of its success suggest some lessons very different from those preached at sportswriters' dinners and locker room prayer meetings.

Consider the essential irony: we live, we are told, in a competitive society, where each individual must strive for excellence on his own merits. But the success of the Celtics is based on a philosophy wholly opposed to individualism. The basic Auerbach commandment is that to win, the individual must fit in; he must subordinate his desires and skills to those of the team. He must, to use an Auerbach watchword, "sacrifice himself," in his life and on the court, to the working of the team. There is something almost subversive about the communal, collective operation of a team like the Celtics. In their encouragement of players to do what they do best and to ask the same of their teammates, there is a dim echo of Marx: "from each according to his abilities, to each according to his needs."

What Auerbach built in Boston has inspired some to wonder what his competitive genius might have done in another, broader field, and whether he chose an arena that was too narrow for his abilities. Clearly, Auerbach's success is based in part on the simple fact that he was smarter than the men he coached against. In picking talent and motivating that talent to perform, he was the best of all professional coaches.

But before making an ideal of the man, we must recognize the limits of his achievement: the success of an organization like the Celtics is only possible in an arena as limited and as artificial as sports. Sports has, for instance, a body of rules that everyone agrees on, so that superior talent is not challenged by fraud or deceit or outright violence. Coaches like Auerbach constantly talk about the gamesmanship that takes place on the court—hooking an opponent's shirt, hectoring referees—but compared to the real world athletic competition is on a level of honor unimaginable elsewhere. The sports teams do not bribe referees, for example, or refuse to obey the calls of officials, or send goon squads out to beat up the opposition's best player in his home, or try to field six or seven men against another team's five. These are ludicrous examples; they could not possibly happen in big-time athletics, no matter how fierce the competition. But they occur every day in the "real" world of government, politics and finance. When the final whistle blows on the court, everyone knows the score. Rarely in our lives is that true.

Sports also defies decay. Every year there are new young men with tireless bodies, ready to take up where their aging elders of twenty-eight and thirty-two leave off. In almost every other part of our lives, we are surrounded by people who have aged their way into prominence; in government, particularly in the Congress, venerability is by itself a road to power. But throughout Auerbach's quarter-century-long tenure in Boston, he has never had to face the prospect of diminishing faculties, except to recognize what element of his team needed replacing (it was his failure to plan for that event in the case of Bill Russell that was largely responsible for Boston's one losing season). Auerbach is now a sixty-year-old grandfather, gray-haired where he is not bald, but on the court the players are always young.

Indeed, there is but one other arena where these conditions —respect for the rules of the game and "eternal youth"— apply, and that is the classroom. Auerbach started out his career with the goal of being a teacher, and there is a fair case to be made that this is exactly what he became. He withdrew from the real world for the comfortable security of a sheltered arena; he developed a theory which in turn spawned a generation of disciples; and he encouraged his players to get the most out of themselves. The role of Mr. Chips is a role that Auerbach, who revels in being tough-guy, would deny playing. But to those who know him, and who know him as "a soft-hearted, sentimental old slob" under the gruffness, Mr. Chips is close to the mark.

For me, the Celtic achievement is a benchmark, a tool to measure a set of unhappy failures. We have lived through a time in which nothing seems to be working any more—not government, not business, not the values of home or work or church. Our homilies, our cherished truths, have been battered by tales of corruption. In the world of sports, the homilies are easier to live by. Yet it still requires brains and skill to transmit values in sports. And Auerbach succeeded so well that the older players have passed the Celtic traditions on to teams far and wide. It is just this kind of shared value system that seems to have disappeared from our own lives.

The Celtics today are flourishing as they have been for

more than twenty years. They are in substantial measure the creation of one man, Red Auerbach. The sad part of this story is that we in other walks of life must look to the limited world of sport to celebrate a success that is both genuine and honorable.

About the Author

Jeff Greenfield is a free-lance writer and political consultant. He has written for many leading magazines and is a contributing editor to *Sport*. He also served as an assistant to Senator Robert Kennedy and Mayor John Lindsay of New York and is co-author (with Jack Newfield) of *A Populist Manifesto*. He lives in New York City and roots for the Knicks despite his admiration for the Celtics.